Griffin Gorge Associates, LLC
Glenville, New York

Copyright 2018
All Rights Reserved
ISBN: 9781791958299
MET Version III

GriffinGorge@mail.com

GriffinGorge.com

No part of this program may be used or reproduced without written permission from Griffin Gorge Associates.

Except:

1. The section on Problem Solving which is from the US Army's Combined Arms Staff Services School and is in the public domain.

2. Users are encouraged to copy the formatted Objectives & Actions Plan worksheet, Briefings and Operations Plan for their use.

Email us to request:

1. Copies of our Objectives & Action Plan spreadsheet.

2. Word document or a PDF for the Problem Solving outline, Guidance Brief, Decision Brief and Operations Plan.

3. Our current course listing and prices.

Griffin Gorge Associates
To Sell Merchandise At A Profit

Introduction
   Preface   1
   1. Levels Of Influence   3
   2. Task & Purpose   7
   3. The Operational Level Retail Manager's
       Primary Task & Purpose   8
   4. Money   9
   5. Moving Merchandise Is An Outstanding
       Community Service Function   10
   6. Mission Essential Tasks (MET)   10
   7. The 12 Mission Essential Tasks   11
   8. Just Don't Suck   13
   9. Leadership   14

MET 1 Planning
   1. Introduction   16
   2. Set A Goal   17
   3. Objectives   18
   4. After Objectives   22
   5. Action Plans   23
   6. Battle Rhythm   26
   7. Managing Suspense's   29
   8. Continuity Binder   30
   9. Definitions   31

MET 2 Staff
   1. Introduction   32
   2. Personalities   34
   3. Disabilities   36

   Part I The Leaders You Follow
   1. The Strategic Office   38
   2. Your Boss   38
   3. Translate Their Directions Into Action   39
   4. Provide Valuable Feedback   40

   Part II The Staff You Lead
   1. Select Your Staff   41
   2. Train Your Staff   45
   3. Direct Your Staff   47
   4. Develop Your Staff   50
   5. Reward Your Staff   53
   6. Collaborate With Peers   53
   7. Conclusion   54

MET 3 Customer Service
    1. Introduction   55
    2. Seven Steps To Retail Customer Service   56
    3. Conclusion   67

MET 4 Community
    1. Introduction   68
    2. The Binder   68
    3. After The Binder   70
    4. Conclusion   71

MET 5 Merchandise
    1. Introduction   72
    2. The Correct Product Mix   72
    3. Your Staff Are The Product Experts   73

MET 6 Inventory Management
Part I. Accountability Of The Merchandise   76
    1. Receiving   76
    2. Front End   77
    3. Records   77
    4. Inventory Day   78

Part II. Managing The Flow Of The Merchandise
    1. Introduction   80
    2. Map Your Section Sales   80
    3. Plan For Your Orders   81
    4. Sell From A Full Floor   82
    5. Stockroom Management   82
    6. Conclusion   83

MET 7 Selling Floor
    1. Introduction   84
    2. Map The Floor   84
    3. Make Impressions   85
    4. Drive Your Strategic Efforts   86
    5. Floor Checklists   86

MET 8 Competition
    1. Introduction   90
    2. The Threat   90
    3. Study The Competition   91
    4. Industry Trends   92
    5. Conclusion   93

MET 9 Loss Prevention
1. Introduction — 94
2. Employee Accidents — 95
3. Utility Bills — 95
4. Lean Six Sigma Principles — 96
5. Returns — 97
6. Employee Theft — 98
7. Employee Attentiveness — 100
8. Thieves — 101
9. Listen To The Staff — 102

MET 10 Problem Solving
1. Introduction — 103
2. Process Overview — 104

The Problem Solving Steps
3. Identify The Problem — 105
4. Leadership Guidance — 108
5. Analyze The Problem — 110
6. Develop Courses Of Action (COA) — 111
7. Define The Rating Criteria — 112
8. Compare Courses Of Action — 114
9. Decision Brief — 115

Take Action
10. Write The Operations Plan — 119
11. Implement The Plan — 127
12. Conclusion — 127

MET 11 Ethics
1. Introduction — 129
2. Ethics With Your Staff — 130
3. Ethics With Your Customers — 131
4. Ethics With Your Leadership — 132
5. Ethical Behavior Is A Learned Trait — 132
6. Ethics Is Not About Following The Rules — 133
7. Wells Fargo - A Case Study — 135
8. The Touchy Subject Of Your Staff And Ethics — 136
   Or - Penises, Vaginas And Hormones
9. Venting & Gossip — 138
10. Diversity — 139
11. Conclusion — 140

MET 12 Focus On Yourself

1. Introduction 141
2. Positive Outlook 141
3. Communicate Clearly 142
4. Engage In Learning 142
5. Well Nourished 143
6. Exercise 144
7. Mentally Fit 145
8. Grooming 146
9. Relationships 146
10. Personal Finances 147
11. Build A Personal Set Of Goals, Objectives And Battle Rhythm 148
12. Conclusion 148

Footnotes 149

Bibliography 151

Services Offered By Griffin Gorge Associates 152

PREFACE

Target Audience:

This is a companion book to our training program designed for retail District Managers and Store Managers.

Assistant Store Managers aspiring to manage their own store would gain from this program. Also, the Regional and Home Office leaders would benefit from understanding this program's tenants.

Applicability:

This program is for any retailer that offers goods and services to the public through a brick and mortar establishment. A storefront where customers walk through a door and are greeted by your staff. You can be from a big box retailer, grocery store, or convenience store. You can be a small general store in the Adirondack Mountains, a local plumbing store or a new chain getting off the ground.

Griffin Gorge's Task:

Our task is to provide a program with a series of classes to train, coach and mentor retail District Managers and Store Managers.

Griffin Gorge's Purpose:

The purpose is to guide your Operational Level leadership into achieving a sustainable sales increase with a corresponding gain to profits.

Griffin Gorge Associates

**We coach your retail leaders to succeed
in growing their business sales and profits.**

Griffin Gorge's Corporate Goal:

Our corporate Goal is to provide top tier training to our customers and to grow our staff of instructors as we expand the business. Our expansion will only happen by selecting top-talent for our instructors. These instructors are our key element in providing a service to our customers. The growth will come when our customers are succeeding by putting our training program into action.

Griffin Gorge Associates
To Sell Merchandise At A Profit

Methodology & Background

Our methodology is to transcribe the military deliberate planning and decision-making process to retail store operations. These principles are proven to be effective in leading small and large teams through complex operations.

Training for District and Store Managers, if it even exists beyond anything informal, often does not provide concrete methodologies that have been tried, tested and refined. These managers are intelligent dedicated individuals striving to achieve the best results for their company. With the proper training, they will achieve even more than they believed they could.

Griffin Gorge Associates is a group of instructors that have a background in retail and military planning. This combined experience allows us to tailor the planning and decision making process to meet your needs. We have an understanding of your business because we are in your business. We have also planned and conducted military operations during peacetime training exercises, overseas operations to include combat, military responses to disasters in the US, and led significant organizational changes within the military.

Our employment in the civilian sector identified a gap that most retailers face. There are many hard working intelligent leaders who have not had the training to give them focus to their efforts. We built this program to remedy that issue.

Our program is designed to build your retail District Manager and Store Manager's development through the Mission Essential Tasks of planning, problem solving, staffing and store operations. The result will be increased sales with a corresponding increase in profit margins.

> **"They are not stupid.**
> **These are intelligent people who have not been trained."**
>
> **Commander Kevin Ettrich, United States Navy**

Introduction

This introduction provides the foundation for the program. Here we define roles, establish definitions and set the stage before getting into the 12 Mission Essential Tasks of a successful store.

1. LEVELS OF INFLUENCE

There are three levels of influence for a retail store. In most cases, they are geographically and structurally separated. A small chain of stores or a single store will certainly have the three levels, however they will be scaled down to a smaller level. This workbook is geared towards a store where they are geographically and structurally separated.

This program is structured towards a retail store on the **Operational Level**.

```
STRATEGIC LEVEL
 The Home Office
 ─────────────
 Vision: 1-5 Years
```

```
        OPERATIONAL LEVEL
         District Manager
          Store Managers
         ─────────────
      Vision: 1 Month to 1 Year
```

```
              TACTICAL LEVEL
              Customer Interface
              ─────────────
           Vision: NOW to 1 Month
```

There is a **Geo-Political Level** above the Strategic Level. This deals with influencing legislation, governing agencies and other countries.

There is also a **Theater Level** in multi-national organizations; example a South American or Asian Office.

For this program, these two Levels are not discussed.

A. **Strategic Level**

Vision: 1-5 years

The Strategic Level is the home office. It is responsible for setting guidance and general direction for the company. Their function is to look at what the company will be doing 1-5 years out. They set plans in motion to bring the company forward.

They are concerned with:

- Product (what the stores are going to offer: fishing tackle, paint, clothes)
- Buying contracts for the merchandise & product pricing
- Store locations (east coast, west coast, in malls or free standing)
- Distribution networks
- Advertising & marketing
- Payroll, pension plans and human resource policies
- Finance & accounting
- Investor relations and seeking capital to grow
- Legal concerns
- Regulations

Introduction

B. Operational Level

Vision: 1 month to 1 year

The Operational Level is where we have the District Managers and the Store Managers.

The Operational Level bridges the gap between the Strategic and Tactical Levels.

> **The Operational Level**
> Takes the Strategic Level direction
> and turns that into action on the Tactical Level.

This program is designed to train the Operational Level leaders into realizing their full potential. A company will thrive or fail based on the quality of its Operational Level talent. As a group, the Operational leaders are absolutely the key to a profitable business. The Operational team has a direct influence on the quality and performance of the Tactical Level.

At the Operational Level your real focus is from next month through one-year out. Sure, you will have issues and problems that are of the daily flavor. But your main focus is to resolve the one month to one year issues and problems. Backwards planning is the path forward.

You will look at your Strategic Level guidance, develop guidance for your subordinates, anticipate your constraints and see where you want to be in one year from now. You will then develop Objectives and Action Plans to get there.

C. **Tactical Level**

Vison: Now to 1 month

This is where your business interacts directly with the customer. This is a retail store at the individual or team level. A short list of focus areas include:

- The opening manager getting the store ready for the day
- The receiving team unloading a truck
- Re-stocking the shelves
- Answering the telephone
- Putting up new displays
- Interviewing for new cashiers
- Adjusting the schedule for call-outs
- Showing the customer add-on sales they need
- Bringing the customer a cart
- The front end manager working the lines
- The casher ringing out a customer
- The closing manager going through their cash out procedures
- Mopping the floor and cleaning the potties at the end of the day

Introduction

2. TASK & PURPOSE

Everything you do is driven by a Task-Purpose. This provides a clear succinct way to state what needs to be done and importantly, why you are doing it. Allow the person doing the task to figure out *how* to do it - they just might surprise you in a good way.

<u>TASK</u>
What are you doing?

<u>PURPOSE</u>
Why are you doing it?

Tasks & Purposes are often nested. You have a Primary Task & Purpose with several sub Tasks and Purposes that allow you to accomplish the Primary. These sub Tasks-Purposes are building blocks for the Primary Task-Purpose.

> **Primary Task:** Take a sip of fine scotch
> **Purpose:** To feel relaxed at the end of a long month

> **Sub-Task:** Go to the store
> **Purpose:** To buy a bottle of scotch

> **Sub-Task:** Go to work
> **Purpose:** To earn some greenbacks

NOTE: Another way of nesting these is to use a Program Evaluation Review Technique (PERT) diagram or the Critical Path Method. This is not covered in our program. If requested, our instructors are qualified to teach this.

When you are directing your staff you must be clear in communicating the Task and giving them the Purpose. These should be short and simple statements using action verbs. If you receive communication from your leadership, seek to get a clear Task-Purpose by asking questions if you do not understand.

Your primary Task-Purpose will be translated to your Goal.

3. THE OPERATIONAL LEVEL RETAIL MANAGER'S PRIMARY TASK & PURPOSE

Primary Task:	To Sell Merchandise
Purpose:	To Make A Profit

This gets translated to be your GOAL:

To Sell Merchandise At A Profit.

That's it. That is the sole reason for opening your doors in the morning. Your existence is based on selling your merchandise and services at a profit.

This goal should apply to every retail store. Every day. Every year.

Now let's break this down.

Customer Service is not your primary Task-Purpose or Goal.

In many places and in many industries that serve customers, there are a lot of smart individuals that state their goal is to provide outstanding customer service.

Is your *Task* to provide super great outstanding customer service with a *Purpose* to have them love you?

If that is the case, when a customer comes in, help them load up a cart, pack it chock full of great items, walk RIGHT past the register and wave. Hang the curtains they just purchased, put together the bookshelf, iron the shirts. That is some great customer service. No doubt they are telling all their friends how wonderful your store is. You are not going to be around long in this scenario. You will have happy customers, but the profit margins will not be sustainable (actually - there would be no profit margins). You will die as a business but they will talk good about you for years to come.

You need good customer service but it's not your goal. It is not your primary Task-Purpose.

It is BY providing great customer service you will get them to part with their money and come back to do it again. Customer service a means to get to your Goal - but it is not your Goal.

Do not confuse your Goal with the Objectives needed to get to your Goal.

Customer Service is an Objective that helps you achieve your Goal.
(More on this in Mission Essential Task 3 - Customer Service).

4. MONEY

That is what you are really after.

The money belongs to the customer and you need to take it from them. Get their money.

But they are not going to just roll up, drop the money off and go away.

Just like you are not going to give everything away for free - the customer is not going to give up his money without something in exchange.

You need to earn it. You need to provide a product, service and shopping experience that is worth the money they spend. And they will be back. And you can take their money again. What a great cycle of events you can create.

Selling and making a profit.

The first indicator of a successful retail store is the revenue generated. How much money are you taking in? Higher receipts at the end of the day means you just might be succeeding. High revenue means you stand a chance at a high profit.

GOOD SALES COVER A LOT OF SINS

You can make a few mistakes and high sales will mask them. If you have low sales, even small mistakes stand out.

INCREASE YOUR SALES VOLUME

    MOVE YOUR MERCHANDISE

Move that merchandise from the loading dock onto your shelves, into the customers carts, go through the registers (take their money) and send them out the door.

5. MOVING MERCHANDISE IS AN OUTSTANDING COMMUNITY SERVICE FUNCTION

Understand what good things come from moving merchandise into your community.

You are providing for people. When you are selling your merchandise at a profit - you are making a better community and raising the standard of living for a lot of others around you.

Look at what you are selling. The customers NEED you to provide merchandise and services. Customers need sheets and towels. Customers need curtains (many of their neighbors would like them to have curtains). Customers need shirts, food, toiletries, shoes, lumber, and paint.

Most people in the developed world today live better than 97.65% of the people that ever walked this planet.

Why?

Because we can buy things to improve our station in life.

After a disaster, one of the key factors during the recovery phase is getting the stores operating so they can provide merchandise and services to the public. This is evident by the fact that FEMA uses the Waffle House Index (WHI) to measure the effects of disasters. The WHI measures how many Waffle Houses are open after a natural disaster. After a disaster you work to save lives, clear roads, restore power and open the stores.

Get the stores open!

> **Running your store is a key element of the community**

If you can grow while making a profit - You are successful.

6. MISSION ESSENTIAL TASKS (MET)

Once the Goal has been defined, the next step is defining the collective set of tasks that will drive you towards that Goal. Mission Essential Tasks are a set of collective tasks that a business strives to be proficient in. This will give the company focus on where to expend their resources. The METs will enable the company to operate with a unity of effort. All of the Operational Level leaders are driving their efforts in the same direction. The Strategic level can influence this direction by giving guidance through the defined framework.

Introduction

METs are used to standardize the employment of resources throughout the company while allowing flexibility for leaders on the Operational Level.

Each MET is comprised of a broad collection of sub-tasks. The military term for these sub-tasks is a Mission Essential Task List (METL). In this book, we do not dig deep in drafting out a complete set of METLs. Here, we just provide an overview of the METs. Detailed METLs are specific to each company, since it will incorporate their unique practices. Griffin Gorge does provide a service to develop a METL for your company.

7. THE 12 MISSION ESSENTIAL TASKS

There are 12 Mission Essential Tasks that drive success at the Operational Level when running a retail store. Which one of these is more important is like asking which is more important - your heart or your lungs? All are needed to get through the day. Taken together, they bring the store to life. They sustain the store for long term growth.

MET 1 Planning
Set about 10-12 Objectives for the year that will guide your store to your Goal (*To Sell Merchandise At A Profit*). Write out an Action Plan for each Objective, detailing the tasks needed to achieve success. Make a Battle Rhythm to keep you focused and on schedule. This MET becomes the brains of your operation. Ensure you put semi-regular review points on the calendar as necessary to monitor progress and allow for readjustment.

MET 2 Staff
Your most important asset. These are the people that will put your Plans into action. Also, you are part of the staff for the Strategic Office. Understand the role you play for each.

MET 3 Customer Service
You need to invest in customer service. A successful store is able to take the customer's money and have them feel good about it.

MET 4 Community
Understanding the world around you. Know your community. These are the people that shop in your store and the staff you hire.

MET 5 Merchandise
This is the stock and services you sell. Develop the right product mix for your stores. While most of this is controlled at the Strategic Level, you do need to influence it where possible. Then, develop product training for your staff so they become the experts.

MET 6 Inventory Management
Millions of dollars of inventory pass through your store. Proper handling and accounting for the merchandise is a cornerstone for making a profit. <u>Those that can master the flow of merchandise into the store will see the greatest sales increases.</u> You need to know how to manage your inventory for seasonal variations. Keep the shelves full.

MET 7 Selling Floor
Your selling floor is a stage in an elaborate production. You need to produce an awesome show. We emphasize checklists that will guide you to keeping a selling floor in good order.

MET 8 Competition
A customer can purchase any product and service you sell from someone else nearby or on-line. As Sun Tzu said "You need to understand the enemy better than yourself." This will allow you to defeat your competition.

MET 9 Loss Prevention
Loss Prevention is more than preventing a crackhead from stealing a shirt. You take lots of money into your registers. You take money out to pay salaries, pay the vendors, the utility companies and other costs. That is money invested because you are getting something in return. When you spend money or manpower on something that does not offer a return, it is a loss. You need to recognize where you are losing money and how to prevent it.

MET 10 Problem Solving
There is a detailed (and painful) planning methodology called the Military Decision Making Process (MDMP). It goes through steps to solve a problem, make a decision and develop a plan. We have adapted this process to be less painful and more responsive to serve your needs. Learning how to problem solve and make the best decision available is a valuable lesson for anyone.

MET 1 Ethics
Unethical behavior is like pornography. Hard to define but most people know it when they see it. We train people with the simple statement - If it sounds right; it's probably right. If it sounds wrong; it's probably wrong. As a leader, you need to set an example for ethically sound behavior to keep the trust of your leadership, your staff, your peers, your customers and most importantly, your family. You must also reinforce positive ethical behavior and build a culture that fosters long-term success.

MET 12 Focus on Yourself
You need to set your own personal goals with objectives to accomplish them. It is important that you work on your self-development to grow personally and professionally. Keep your family life in good repair. You are a leader. You need to lead and set the example.

Introduction

Look at these 12 Mission Essential Tasks. You might notice something that is very important that is missing. The Profit & Loss (P&L) statement is not listed. Your P&L statement is very important. It is NOT one of the 12 Mission Essential Tasks. Your P&L is the metric. It is the statement that shows your sales are going up and you are doing it profitably.

You don't pass a semester of school by studying your report card. You use the report card to identify your successes and areas for improvement. These 12 Mission Essential Tasks will lead you to a successful retail store. Follow this series and you will succeed at selling your merchandise.

You cannot fail when you are operating using this guide. Just no way. If you are just good (no need to be a super hero) on ALL of these you will win.

8. JUST DON'T SUCK

You do not have to be top of the line in everything you do. Just don't suck in anything and you might just end up better than those around you.

You are kidding everyone - including yourself - if you say you are going to give 110% to everything. First of all, you work in retail. This is not an industry known to over hire. You leave at the end of a long day with most stuff not done.

> **If you leave at the end of the day and say everything is done**
> ------
> **You are delusional, clueless, or lying OR all three.**

You are not going to do everything at even at 80%. In fact - to succeed sometimes you only need not to suck. Sure, it is great to be great. Everyone loves to hear stories where the customer is awed by the salesman and they come back to buy even more. Everyone would like to brag that ALL of their customers are blown away by the impressive display of merchandise every time they walk down your aisles. And you do need at least some of these stories to be successful.

What is the reality? The real expectation?

You walk into a store, you find what you need. It is at a reasonable price, you walk up to the register. Pay. The cashier smiles and thanks you. You go to your car and drive away. Not an outstanding event you write home about. You simply needed something, bought it and moved on. The store might not have been GREAT, but it surely did not suck. In the military terms; you do not need to be outstanding in all events, you just need to be proficient in all events.

In the Army we had to take a physical fitness test

This consisted of three events: Pushups, sit ups and a 2 mile run. Points are awarded based on your age and gender. There's a formula. You need a minimum of 60 points in each event to pass. 100 points per event was the maximum score. So- if you got a 60 in all three events you passed the test. There is a mandatory comment on your evaluation with a simple drop down choice to select. It states simply "pass" or "fail."

If you got a 100 points in the pushups, then a 100 points in the sit-ups, and you get 59 points in the run you fail the entire test.

In fact - You could set a world record for the most pushups ever in two minutes, followed by another world record for the most sit-ups a human being has ever done in two minutes. You go forth and miss the 2 mile run by ONE second - you fail. Your evaluation is posted with a fail. Your evaluator will be mandated to formally council you on your failure to meet the minimum physical fitness standards. He is barred from making any positive comment regarding your two world records.

To pass for the year you need 60% in each of the 12 Mission Essential Tasks.

Strive to get a 60 in each of these 12 Mission Essential Tasks, pick out a few to get that 90 or 100. You don't need to be aces in all events - just don't suck in any one of them.

You do need to find your talent, your company's talent and work to excel on at least a few areas. Get a passing grade in all - shine in a few.

District Managers need to balance the talent between their stores. Look at what talent gaps you have and use this as a selection criteria for hiring or promoting new managers.

Work to be proficient in all of the 12 Mission Essential Tasks. You will have a store that is selling a lot of merchandise at a profit.

9. LEADERSHIP

You can go to the library and you can checkout ten books on leadership. They will give fifty different definitions - and none of them are wrong.

Defining what leadership is and what a successful leader does will change on what the mission is and the angle of the view.

But many can agree on what leadership is not.

Leadership is not pretending to be like Patton, riding on top of a tank barreling across the desert with your troops all cheering behind you. That's a Hollywood director selling a show.

Introduction

> **A leader is one who can effectively guide their staff to accomplish the goals and the mission of the company.**

On the Operational Level - a great leader is the diminutive young lady sitting at her desk meticulously working on her Objectives, Action Plans and Battle Rhythm. She is taking the Strategic Office's policy and guidance and breathing life into it. She directs her staff through coaching. She plans a schedule well in advance. She communicates her directions to the assistant managers. She guides her staff through effective performance plans and appraisals. She rewards the performers. She weeds out the poor performers. She sets a standard of ethical practices. She is on her game when directing the flow of merchandise into the store.

She walks the selling floor listening to the staff and customers. She has a dynamic selling floor with eye popping presentations. She communicates back to her home office. Seeking clarification when needed. Providing them feedback on what is working or what needs improvement. She quickly replies to emails from her District Manager. She is leading her staff and her company into selling merchandise at a profit.

That leader who rides on top of a tank shouting "Follow Me" with his troops shouting RAH RAH RAH - but does not sit down to draft coherent plans and write solid performance reviews - is nothing more than an actor putting on a dangerous show.

District Managers and Store Managers - you are leaders that need to properly lead.

> **Do your job**

Griffin Gorge Associates
To Sell Merchandise At A Profit

Mission Essential Task 1
Planning

1. INTRODUCTION

To plan your actions and deployment of resources (staff & funds) in an effort to meet your Strategic Level guidance and build your business towards increased revenue and profit. This MET will increase your ability to earn revenue while conserving resource expenditures that could reduce profits. It synchronizes efforts with the Strategic Office, your boss, peers and subordinates. The Action Plans lay a foundation for your staff to execute with initiative and in concert.

Every District Manager and Store Manager must invest the time to develop Objectives, write solid Action Plans and maintain a Battle Rhythm.

This gives you the focus to reach your Goal.

> WE NEVER FAILED TO FAIL
> IT WAS THE EASIEST THING TO DO
> -CSN[1-1]

If you do not set Objectives, draft Action Plans and develop a Battle Rhythm you are wandering aimlessly.

You are a leader. You are driving your business. Do it with some level of intelligence.

The way we guide you here makes it easy. You're not building a space shuttle. Just invest a little time and you will get there.

Goal > An aim point for your business.

> _Objectives_ > A set of defined actions that collectively guide your business to your Goal. You should end up with about 10 - 12 Objectives to support that.
>
>> _Action Plans_ > The plans for how you will accomplish each Objective. In here, you will assign specific tasks to an individual and direct the resources.

Battle Rhythm > This will keep you focused and on track to meet your Objectives. A time management tool to record the re-occurring events you do:

> - daily
>   - weekly
>   - bi-weekly
>   - monthly
>   - quarterly
>   - semi-annually
>   - annually

Socialize the Battle Rhythm amongst your staff so they can adhere to it.

2. SET A GOAL

A Goal is the aim point for your business. It is something you strive for.

Your Goal is the aim point to which you focus your efforts, manpower, resources and funding. It gives your business a sense of direction. In most cases, you will have a single Goal.

Unlike the Objectives listed below, your Goal is often not defined with a metric. Often it is not a finish line you cross.

As discussed in the Introduction, your Goal:

To Sell Merchandise At A Profit.

The Objectives used to reach your Goal will change.

_____

On the **Strategic Level**, the Home Office will have a different Goal. Their Goal might indicate what market share they want to gain or what financial status the company is trying to achieve. This might include brick & mortar stores with an on-line business.

Possible Strategic Goal: To gain the dominate retail market share for soft goods, while leveraging a profit.

_____

On the **Tactical Level,** a salesman on your selling floor will have yet another Goal. His Goal might be to increase his personal sales. Profit will not be, and should not be, a part of his sphere of influence.

3. OBJECTIVES

Objectives are a collective set of actions that support your Goal. Think of these as a set of sub-goals. Objectives are used to manage and direct your resources (manpower & funds). In a retail store, you should set about 10 - 12 Objectives.

As you develop your Objectives, a single objective will normally incorporate two or more of the 12 Mission Essential Tasks. In the end, with your 10 - 12 Objectives, you want to make sure all of the 12 Mission Essential Tasks are addressed.

A good practice is to set a series of Objectives for each year. Additionally, you will find yourself adding some Objectives during the year. You may also complete an Objective before the year is up.

So what makes for a good objective?

    A. Objectives must **directly support** your Goal. They need to be set in a way that will drive your business to increase revenue and profit.

    B. Objectives must be **well defined**. A short well-defined statement works.

    C. Objectives must be **measurable** in an objective way.

    D. Objectives must be **attainable** with effort. The metric must be more of a prediction. It should not intentionally be lower so you can brag you exceeded it. It should not be so far out it become laughable.

> Use Objectives to guide your store's manpower, resources and funds towards achieving your Goal.

The Objectives must be communicated to your team and understood at the lowest level.

MET 1: Planning

Sample Objectives

A set of sample Objectives that will collectively guide your business to your Goal:

Objective 1
To have a sales increase of 6.2% for the next 12 months.
Note - All stores should have their projected total sales increase as the first Objective.

Objective 2
Increase the sales in the Frame section by 25% over the next 12 months.

Objective 3
Reduce the staff turnover to less than 18% over the next 12 months.

Objective 4
Reduce the costs associated with employee accidents by more than 30% in the next 12 months.

Objective 5
Reduce the man-hours required to unload the trucks by more than 10% over the next 12 months.

Objective 6
Increase the sales of add-on merchandise in the Sporting Goods section by more than 15% in the next 12 months.

Objective 7
To have the year-end shrink be less than .9%.

Objective 8
Complete all employee evaluations before the deadlines.

Objective 9
Increase the sales of the top 10 most profitable items in the store by more than 18% over the next 12 months.

Objective 10
Develop a partnership with the local mattress stores to display bedding ensembles. Projected to increase bedding ensemble sales by more than 20%.

Objective 11
All schedules posted 30 days prior. Less than 10% changes to the schedule once posted.

Griffin Gorge Associates
To Sell Merchandise At A Profit

Setting Objective 1

The first Objective should be to determine your sales increase for the next year.

OBJECTIVE: Increase the store sales by XX.XX % over the next 12 months.

TASK / PURPOSE: Accurately predict the sales increase for the store in order to manage the resources (staff & inventory) to meet the anticipated need.

Make this an intelligent act that accurately predicts where you will end up. Use the following as guide to assist you in getting the right number.

1: Get some history

	3 Years Ago	2 Years Ago	Last Year
Your store sales increase	_____	_____	_____
Sister store sales increase	_____	_____	_____
The district sales increase	_____	_____	_____
The company sales increase	_____	_____	_____
A competitor company sales	_____	_____	_____
National retail sales increase	_____	_____	_____

2. Then look at your staff. Determine if they are trending as a strong team, or do you have a staff that is in a learning curve. Do you anticipate a higher turnover of strong players?

3. Find out what your company is telling the investors. What are the Wall Street projections for national retail sales growth?

4. Look at the trends for the industry you are in.

5. Study the prospects for the economic growth in your community. Check with your local elected officials and librarian.

6. Add some of your intuition about the potential for your store. You should be able to take all of this to get a pretty good projected sales increase for the next year.

Once you have this estimate, use it as a guide when ordering your merchandise. Don't under-estimate this so you look like a hero at the end of the year by beating your projection. You need to feed the beast. You cannot grow by ordering the same amount of merchandise as last year. Don't over-estimate - you will be feeding your stockrooms. Use this as a guide for hiring into your staff.

MET 1: Planning

A Collective Event

You should not develop your Objectives in a vacuum. Start by developing just four or five on your own.

Then go to your supervisor. Show her what you are developing. Discuss your reasons for each one. Ask her for input and feedback.

Then, go around to your staff and get their comments. Show them what you have developed. Ask a few key members what they would like to see added. Ask them for ways to increase sales or profits. Your peers should be developing Objectives. Share ideas amongst each other.

With the added input from your boss, staff and peers, you should come out with your 10 - 12 Objectives.

Your Evaluation

Before you dig into the details and write Action Plans, take your final list of Objectives to your boss. You must have a deliberate face to face discussion about how these Objectives will achieve your Goal and support the guidance from the Strategic Office.

This becomes the foundation for your Performance Evaluation. You have set a solid plan with measurable results. If you meet all of these - your Boss has no choice but to give you an outstanding evaluation.

(Mission Essential Task 12 - Focus on Yourself)

Flexible Objectives

Always be flexible with your Objectives. Remember - their purpose is to guide your business towards the Goal. However, circumstances and conditions often change and you may need to reevaluate the Objectives as situations dictate.

Reasons to change or end work on an Objective:

- The circumstances change and it no longer supports your Goal.
- The resources required are no longer available or cost more than the expected return.
- You developed a better avenue to achieve the outcome.
- Adjustments to accommodate loss or gain of staff members.
- Significant policy shifts from Strategic Office.
- Analysis indicates a better course is to combine or split Objectives.
- After review, you decide it just is not a good Objective.
- You met the Objective.

4. AFTER OBJECTIVES

Once you have a set of Objectives, the real hard part starts. The Objectives will not just happen. **You now need to do the hard part of leadership.** Sit down in a quiet space and start to map out how you will guide your organization to reach those Objectives. You need to communicate, direct resources, establish priorities, set suspense's, and allow flexibility.

You will do this by writing out an Action Plan for each Objective. We have an easy to fill in template for your use. It is an Excel spreadsheet that has one tab for each Objective. There is a front tab that will provide a summary each time an Objective is updated.

This is hard because it takes discipline to sit down and work through these. Remember, you have a staff you are developing. Coach your key staff members to write an Action Plan for you.

The great advantage of an Action Plan:

-You are directing manpower and resources to guide your business. There is a lot of hustle and bustle on your selling floor, the stockrooms and offices of your business. People, and the organization, can easily lose sight of what is important. The Action Plans keep the focus.

-You are communicating. Your store is in operation over 110 hours per week. You are a star if you are there for half of it. The Action Plans provide clear direction to your staff in your absence.

-You are setting priorities. There are too many tasks for your staff to accomplish each week. The Action Plans help to set priorities for their efforts.

-You allow for flexibility. The Action Plans can be adjusted as the year goes by. Circumstances change and you can easily adjust the plan to meet the needs. Also, your staff will come up with better ways to reach the Objective; your Action Plans are built to accept adjustments.

If done correctly, it actually becomes hard to miss your Objectives.

The Objectives and Action Plans are not exclusive.

It would be bury your business in paper if you were to write out an Action Plan for every single task you need to do.

Your list of Objectives and the supporting Action Plans will not encompass everything you need to accomplish. There will be other very important tasks that must be completed. The Objectives are there to guide your efforts; but not at the exclusion of everything else.

MET 1: Planning

5. ACTION PLANS

As an example, we have an Objective to increase the sales of the Frame section by 25% over the next 12 months. This will not happen on its own. You need to direct the resources to shape the events that will increase your sales in this section.

A sample Action Plan using our Excel spreadsheet:

	A	B	C	D	E	F
1	Objective 2	FRAMES				
2	Task	Purpose	Place an increased focus on the presentation and stock in the frame section in order to increase sales in a niche corner of the store. An additional desired outcome will be increased side sales due to advertising for the frames			
3		Objective	In the period 1st of January to the 31st of December, increase sales in the frame section by at least 25% over previous year sales.			
4		Start Date	1-Jan-18			
5		End Date	31-Dec-18			
6		Owner	Wendy			
7						
8	Action Point 1	CLEAN				
9		Task	Place an emphasis on cleaning the frame section			
10		Purpose	To make the Frame section more presentable to the customers. Also, this will allow us to determine the stock to order.			
11		Assigned To	Task	Remarks	Suspense	
12		Wendy	Cleaning party of 8 associates on Sunday February 7th after the store closes.	Coordinate with Asst Store Mgr to select associates, make a detailed plan and list follow-up actions if required.	7-Feb-18	
13		Closing Manager	Perform nightly cleanings	Closing manager will spend extra time straightening the frames	Daily	
14		Scheduler	Identify a person on the schedule to conduct a weekly check to monitor that standards are being kept.	Rotate associates to perform a weekly ch	Weekly	
15		Scheduler	Identify a person on the schedule to conduct periodic dusting on the first and third Monday of each month.		Bi-monthly	
16		Wendy	Cleaning party of 8 associates on Sunday July 1st after	Coordinate with Asst Store Mgr to select	31-Jul-18	
17						
18	Action Point 2	DISPLAYS				
19		Task	Place frame displays around the store and change on a regular schedule			
20		Purpose	To increase customer awareness of our frame section			
21		Assigned To	Task	Remarks	Suspense	
22		Karen	Change displays of frames in the front window on the 2nd and 4th Wednesday of each month.	Coordinate with Wendy on the theme.	Bi-monthly	
23		Nier	Change displays of frames in the front window on the 1st and 3rd Thursday of each month.	Coordinate with Wendy on the theme.	Bi-monthly	
24		Kwami	Change the frames displayed in the aisles.	Location and frequency determined by the Asst Store Mgr.	As requested	
25						

Griffin Gorge Associates
To Sell Merchandise At A Profit

	A	B	C	D	E	F
25						
26	Action Point 3	COUPONS				
27		Task	Target customer base with coupons for frames			
28		Purpose	To generate traffic into the store; specifically towards the frame section			
29		Assigned To	Task	Remarks	Suspense	
30		Store Manager	Contact Rita in the Home Office for initial coupon mailer.	One month after mailer, review redemption rates	1-Mar-18	
31		Miguel	Contact schools listed in Customer Base binder. Request to sponsor events or graduation program guides.	Contact Rita for funding. Work with Wendy for matching displays in the store.	7-Mar-18	
32		Rich	Set up a vendor table at the Old Bridge township stock car races in June. Have a series of action style frames ready to sell.	Have a remote register setup.	15-Jun-18	
33						
34	Action Point 4	STOCK				
35		Task	Increase stock levels in the frame section to include seeking new selections.			
36		Purpose	To support the anticipated increase in sales for the frames.			
37		Assigned To	Task	Remarks	Suspense	
38		Wendy	Conduct visits to the competitors to keep informed of their frame selections and market presence.	Submit a short email on the findings NLT the following day.	Each Tuesday	
39		Asst Store Mgr	Place orders for stock in order to keep the shelves full. Keep a heavier stock of the basic frames.	Review the orders with Wendy in an effort to coordinate the displays and the stock levels.	Bi-weekly	
40		Asst Store Mgr	Review seasonal frames 3 months prior to season.	Ensure stock levels for seasonal frames are adequate. Avoid an over-order that results in markdowns.	Quarterly	
41		Store Manager	Discuss frame sales with District Manager to develop a strategy for six months out.	Review sales history and comparison to sister stores.	Quarterly	
42						

Header Information

Line 1:   The Tile of the Objective
Line 2:   Task/Purpose: Write out what it is you are attempting to do and why
Line 3:   Objective Description: Include timeframe and the measurable
Line 4:   Start Date
Line 5:   End Date
Line 6:   Owner. The person who will have responsibility for the Action Plan

After the header information, you will write out the outline for each Action Point.

Action Points

Take each Objective and develop some Action Points that will get you to reach that Objective.

Action Points are a set of related Tasks that will make a significant contribution to achieving your Objective.

These can be one word to one sentence.

MET 1: Planning

In our example for the Objective FRAMES, the 4 Action Points are:

<u>Clean</u> Your weekend associate suggested the biggest problem was the Frame section looks like a tornado hit it.

<u>Displays</u> You determined that putting displays around the store will help drive traffic to the Frame section.

<u>Coupons</u> The Home Office has agreed to do some coupon mailers to let your customer base know how great your Frame section is. Include some additional outreach and advertising actions.

<u>Stock</u> You want to make sure the Frame section stays stocked. Get ready for that increased traffic.

Line 8: Title of the Action Point
Line 9: Task (What are you doing)
Line 10: Purpose (Why are you doing this)
Line 11:
    Assigned To: Pin the rose on a person or position for this task
    Task: A short sentence on what is to be done
    Remarks: Additional information regarding the task
    Suspense: The date the task needs to be completed or the frequency

Add as many task lines needed for the Action Point. Try to keep this to just 3-6 tasks. Provide just general guidance, this will allow the person assigned the task some flexibility.

Time To Digest And Think About Some Things

Look at the second order of effects here.

- How does this play into turnover? Your part-time weekend employee, Wendy, did not cost more. She now feels like a part of your business. She is invested into the future of your store.

- You have carefully directed the store's resources towards a specific set of actions that will increase your sales.

- You should have confidence that your staff will be able to get this accomplished in your absence.

- You have trained some of the junior staff members on the value of planning.

- Customer base is increasing. Word out on the street is you are the frame destination. Customers come in for frames and leave with a bedding ensemble.

6. BATTLE RHYTHM

Defined: A schedule of activities intended to manage time and synchronize actions.

A Battle Rhythm is a way to keep you focused.

It synchronizes the:

- Suspense's you have from your Strategic Office
- Suspense's from your Boss
- Suspense's you created when writing the Objectives
- Activities you need to perform
- Activities you need to monitor
- Key dates
- Re-occurring events

Time Management

You are busy everyday - every hour. Your well thought out - boss approved - Battle Rhythm is there to keep you focused.

People will be pulling at you all day trying to get your attention for something. You will get phone calls from other stores, your boss, customers, and staff. You will see small and large problems that you want to jump in and fix.

Step back for a second. Your well-developed Objectives and Plans need to move to the front.

As a leader, sometimes the hardest part is learning not to jump in and solve a problem. When you get distracted and go chasing monkeys that are not on your priority list - you are now not working on your priorities.

Let some of the small problems go. Determine what tasks can be dropped and what are the ones that you can delegate.

Challenge and trust your subordinates to solve problems and make decisions.

A Battle Rhythm is designed to assist you with time management.

Your Two Page Battle Rhythm

Get a two week calendar and write in the events that occur across the time, leaving out the Daily events. Two weeks is used since that is the most common pay period.

MET 1: Planning

Example Battle Rhythm

MONDAY	TUESDAY	WEDNESDAY	THURSDAY	FRIDAY	SATURDAY	SUNDAY
Weekly Front End Meeting Send in Payroll	Walk sporting goods area	Home Office call-in 10am Review schedule changes for next pay period	Day Off	Walk floor to check flyer Check-in with DM for suspense's	Walk floor in am	Day Off
Weekly Front End Meeting	Check orders for hard goods	District call-in 10am	Day Off	Check orders for soft goods Inspect stockrooms	Day Off	Work front end in am

Daily

    a. Walk Frame section.

    b. Check receiving area and stockrooms.

    c. Review closing report from previous day.

    d. Clear emails.

Monthly

    a. First week, chart progress on all Objectives. Make notes to discuss with District Manager.

    b. Third week, review all ads for next month.

    c. Walking discussion with each floor manager for the store's Objectives.

Example Battle Rhythm

Quarterly

    a. Check with Rita for coupon mailers.

    b. Managers & Key Leader review of Objectives.

    c. Staffing review with Tina in Human Resources.

Semi-Annual

    a. Interim reviews completed.

    b. Mentoring sessions with key staff.

    c. Formal Objectives review with District Manager.

Annual

    a. Complete staff reviews and set up performance plans for next cycle.

    b. January: Complete Objectives, Action Plans & Battle Rhythm for next year.

Keep the Battle Rhythm posted by your desk. This is specifically designed to keep you focused. It works.

Check it off when you do it.

After a few months you WILL find that you are accomplishing actions listed on your Objectives. Your store is being lead into the direction you planned. You are a professional leader. Your store is focused on growing a profitable business.

MET 1: Planning

8. MANAGING SUSPENSE'S

Managing suspense's is a tough one. There will be a lot of non-recurring suspense's that do not fit into your Battle Rhythm. You must track them to be effective.

Managing the suspense's that you owe your boss or Strategic Office will keep you out of trouble.

Managing suspense's your subordinates owe you will let them know you uphold standards - you run a tight ship.

Use our spreadsheet as a tracker for suspense's. This is a great, and simple, tool used to track what you owe to someone and what your subordinates owe to you.

A Tale of Two Generals
(we use pseudonyms for this one)

General Ricochet-Rabbit loved to shoot from the hip. Going a mile-a-minute, he would tell people to go get something done. He would notoriously send several people out to go get the same task completed. It became comical to stand in front of him getting your tasking. The first thing you did when you walked away was to find the other four Soldiers he told to do the same thing. And- he did this without going through their supervisors.

General Ricochet-Rabbit rarely followed up on his taskings. They were disjointed; reflecting how he felt at the moment and not part of a greater plan. Subordinates picked up on this fast. After you found the other four who were told to work on the same task, the collective thought was to scrap the task and wait for the second request. There were very few second requests. Often, if you did complete the task, he would dismiss you before you could finish telling him. He would give his thanks in a dismissive way.

Then there was General Tracking You. He had a masterful way of tracking everything. You could pass him in the hallway and he would ask about your day. You mention a small issue and the go about your business. A week later, General Tracking You would email you asking if the issue was resolved. If he asked you for something in a meeting; you had better stay on it, because you were guaranteed to get a follow-up email in a month. General Tracking You would build plans for events years ahead. If you asked him about a past event, he would disappear for five minutes and come back with a detailed history.

Those of us working for General Tracking You would wonder what system he used to keep track of all these events and taskings. Nobody ever wondered how General Ricochet-Rabbit tracked his events and suspense's.

Develop a solid way to track your events and taskings. Use our spreadsheet as a starter and adjust it to fit your needs.

9. CONTINUITY BINDER

A Continuity Binder is you writing down what you do, so your replacement can come in a do most of your job. You never know when you will be leaving.

Task: Build a continuity binder that outlines all of the key functions you perform.

Purpose: Serves as a document for your successor to perform the job with having to suffer through a steep learning curve. It ensures your successor does not fail.

Write down what functions you perform and how you do it. It should be written in a way that a manager from another store could come in, read it and pick up where you left off.

<u>Outline</u> is key word here. Just make a short 1-2 page outline of the function. It provides a quick reference on the process and a starting point.

Make a tab for each of the functions you perform:

- Ordering
- Scheduling
- Floor Walks
- Major Events
- Performance Plans
- Sales Tracking
- Seasonal Changeovers
- Customer Interface
- Competition Review
- Sales Review
- Store Map Updates
- Community Review
- Local Officials Interface
- Merchandise Review
- Online Store Review
- Social Media Review
- Loss Prevention Reviews
- Battle Rhythm Updates
- Staff Productivity Reviews
- Customer Service Reviews
- Traffic Flow Pattern Reviews
- District Manager Updates

Place a copy of your Battle Rhythm on the front of the continuity binder. Add some notes to your Battle Rhythm to show why you have something listed.

In here you should keep your Action Plans with some notes on why you chose your Objectives.

This should be updated anytime you have a change. The Continuity Binder is to record how you are doing the technical aspects of your job. It must be flexible and kept current. If you are updating something on it once a week, you are doing it right.

Do not discount the importance of a Continuity Binder. This will ensure success for the next person who comes up behind you. The Continuity Binder removes much of the pain during the learning curve for a new job. District Managers must get every Store Manager to have a Continuity Binder. Store Managers must get each key person to have one.

9. DEFINITIONS

<u>No Earlier Than (NET)</u>: Do not start the task earlier than the date/time specified. You can start later.

<u>No Later Than (NLT)</u>: Complete the task before the date/time specified. You can start earlier.

Example: NET the Tuesday after Labor Day and NLT September 30th, Julie will set up the Halloween section according to the enclosed diagram.

<u>On (date) at (time)</u>: Use when you need to specify an exact date/time for an event
Example: On September 3, at 7:00pm Julie will meet with the Mayor.

<u>Be Prepared To (BPT)</u>: Tells someone to get things ready to do a task, but do not start it until further notice.

Example: Julie will BPT set up the Halloween merchandise in September. The Home Office will not send the exact dates until a month before.

<u>Specified Tasks</u>: A task that is specifically stated in the directions.

<u>Implied Tasks</u>: A task that is not directly communicated in the directions, but will need to be accomplished.

Example: Specified Task in the Action Plan states Julie must drive to another store.

An Implied Task would be that Julie puts fuel in the car.

Mission Essential Task 2
Staff

1. INTRODUCTION

To properly manage the functions of the Staff. Direct your Staff to achieve the guidance from the Strategic Office, your boss and you. The Staff is the most important, and expensive, company resource. This MET centers on properly managing this resource which can potentially provide exponential growth for the company. The dynamics of human personalities and interactions makes this the most difficult aspect of operating a business. Building strong teams in an ever changing environment is difficult and relentless. The principles of leadership involves methods that have been successful in a variety of endeavors. It is through well directed staff development and strong teams that success can be achieved.

In the introduction, leadership was defined as: one who can effectively guide their staff to accomplish the goals and the mission of the company.

Why Is There A Staff?

Your company is in business to make money. It seeks to provide goods or services in return for a profit. Your company employs its people to move the goods and perform services in order to have the customer pay for them. When the business grows, the company needs to hire additional staff to keep pace with the growth. You need people to open and operate new stores and expand your existing ones.

An intelligent growing company hires people to feed the business. A poorly trained dying company will see their stock price increase when they "trim" the payroll.

You Start By Following

In order for you to be a strong leader, you must be following the guidance of your leadership. The reason you are leading your staff is achieve the Goals of your company. If you are not a good follower, you will not be a good leader and you will fail.

You are a District Manager or a Store Manager. You are taking guidance from the Strategic Office and putting that into action.

The Staff You Lead

Once you have established the Objectives, made the Action Plans to accomplish them and drafted a Battle Rhythm to guide you, you need to get your staff to execute it. One way of looking at it - the reason your staff exists is to work on your plans and follow your Battle Rhythm in an effort to meet your Objectives.

MET 2: Staff

You have developed a great set of Action Plans to move your business in the right direction. The next step is to select, train, direct, develop, and reward your staff in the efforts to meet those ends.

- ➤ **Select:** Recruit, interview and hire the right people for the job.

- ➤ **Train:** Provide your staff with the right knowledge and skills to be productive.

- ➤ **Direct:** Guide the actions of your staff through the Action Plans and schedules.

- ➤ **Develop**: Find the talents and desire of your staff and cultivate that to grow your business. This is accomplished formally through the evaluation system and informally through coaching. Identify weaknesses as well as talents.

- ➤ **Reward:** Your staff works hard for you; provide them a return on their investment and you will see both the individual and the company grow.

All Staff Must Be Engaged In Two Primary Functions:

- ➤ **Earning:** Performing a function that will result in a sale or supports the sale. This includes:

  - Moving the goods to stock the shelves
  - Paying the invoices so vendors send more
  - Cleaning the store to be presentable for the customer
  - Updating store displays
  - Cashiers ringing up the sale
  - Engagement with customers for sales

- ➤ **Loss Prevention:** Performing a function that will prevent a loss to the business; qualified by the statement that the cost in performing the function is less that the anticipated loss.

  - Locking the doors at night
  - Regulatory requirements to prevent fines
  - Maintaining a security system
  - Processing returns to vendors

When directing your staff, you must be able to identify if an action is supporting earnings or preventing loss. Some functions such as cleaning an area can be dual purpose. A clean store makes for a more pleasant shopping experience and will reduce theft. Understanding which function your tasks full under will assist you in focusing your limited resources towards accomplishing your Objectives.

_____

Here are some factors to look at when managing and leading your staff.

2. PERSONALITIES

Every single person is different.

All personality traits exist. There is not one person who has a personality trait that is so unique, they are the only individual to ever have it. Traits and motivations are hundreds of thousands of years old. What makes us unique is the combinations of these traits. Each person gets the combination shuffled in different order.

There are 52 cards in a deck.

Suppose each card represents a personality trait. Depending on how they are shuffled and the order, you get a resulting personality that is so unique - nobody has ever had that combination

Shuffle the Deck and the possible combinations are:

80,658,175,943,878,571,660,636,856,403,766,975,289,505,440,883,277,824,000,000,000,000.

There have only been 107,000,000,000 people that ever walked this planet (just a best estimate - we never did get all their names).

The four of clubs represents an irrational fear of something. Many millions have this trait. But mix it with the six of diamonds which is a passion for orderliness and a Jack of hearts which is a gift of storytelling; and so on - you now have a person so unique there has never and will never be another one.

There are more than 52 personally traits - so the possible combinations are even greater.

A personality changes based on how dominate or recessive a trait is. Some traits get dealt from the top of the deck. Some traits stay buried and never get dealt.

You need to move the personalities and talent around to match your needs; the needs of your company. You will not win by pushing a square peg in a round hole.

A skillful leader can understand the differences in people's personalities and use that to build strong teams.

THE STORY OF SUE

Sue was hired for a chain opening a store in a new market. She was given the task to train the cashiers and set up the front end registers. She was remarkable. Her work was very meticulous and thorough. She was the kind of the person you need to run the front end.

Once the store opened, her leadership started having problems with her. The store had a policy to give cash back on returns under $20 with or without a receipt. It was just easier than paying a cashier and front end manager to fill out forms while a line was stacking up.

Quickly, the cashiers learned that the managers would be lenient and give up to $25. A $19.99 item was $21.59 with the tax.

There was a different standard when Sue was on duty. $20.01 without a receipt was over $20. She would have the cashier make the customer fill out forms and present some identification. The store manager had to talk to Sue and tell her it was alright to go a little over. Sue could not grasp that. She twitched. Her mind thought only in black and white. She could not conceptualize a gray area. Is the limit $20 or $21.59? Or $25.00? This was just a small example of many problems.

Sue was the nut in the fruit salad.

It became pretty bad and she was almost removed. Then the receiving manager, Sparky, got promoted to another position. Julie came up to the store manager and made a pretty good suggestion. She suggested they move Sue to the receiving manager position. Phenomenal. Now she could be operating in black and white. Schedule trucks and receiving clerks. Count the boxes and check invoices. Stack things up in the right spot. The store shrink dropped as a direct result of her actions. Sue got a raise.

Understand the differences in people's personalities and learn to use that to benefit both you and the employee.

> **When there is a nut in your fruit salad pick it out and toss it in a nut bowl;**
> **Not the trash**

3. DISABILITIES

Many people have disabilities and some of them are obvious.

Working in a home improvement store was a guy named Jim. If your personality trait for observation was low in your deck of cards, you would still notice something different about Jim.

Jim was in a wheelchair. He weighed about 90 pounds. He had straps to keep his legs from flying around when he wheeled around corners. You would observe Jim and think - he's in a wheelchair and those things look like toothpicks. Then you are hit with the realization - Jim probably cannot walk.

Jim was fantastic at his job. Independent contractors were hired to install various items for the customers. Salesmen made the sale, then Jim did the coordination for the installation. He was a master at setting expectations for the customer and ensuring quality work from the contractors. Anyone in the business can attest this is a tough job to master. Jim made the store a lot of money.

Gary had a disability that was not noticeable. As it happened, Gary worked in the same store with Jim. Gary worked in a hardware section. He was an encyclopedia of knowledge. His mechanical ability was unsurpassed. His work on the selling floor and talking to the customers was a pretty good deal for the business. A customer came in once to ask for a particular and strange item. Gary asked him what it was for. The customer stated he had an old printing press he was trying to revive. Gary's eyes lit up and asked if it was an old Heidelberg press. The customer said yes and Gary was off to the races. He asked what year it was made. Gary found exactly what the customer needed and discussed, in great detail, about some other things to look at when fixing it up. Gary performed feats like that several times a week.

However, Gary had some issues. He was not good with any type of pressure. Seriously had issues. He could be committed to the psych ward if he felt any kind of pressure to accomplish something.

The store leadership learned to work with Gary and his problem. He was never assigned any task. He certainly was never given something with a deadline. If you treated Gary like other employees, Gary would literally go off the deep end.

You would not ask Jim to run up the stairs - that would be cruel to ask a wheelchair bound man to run up the stairs. You would never ask Gary to meet a deadline - that would be just as cruel.

But both Jim and Gary made significant contributions to the company. Learn to spot someone with disabilities in an effort to work with them to be productive employees.

MET 2: Staff

> **You should not treat all employees the same
> BUT
> You do need to be fair to all employees**

Anyone who states they treat all their employees, or all people, the same is in need of some leadership training.

PART I The Leaders You Follow

Being a leader starts with following. You are part of the staff for the Strategic Office. Understand the role you play and the obligations you have.

You are the face that bends the vision and plans from the Strategic Office into action on the Tactical Level.

Earlier, we defined leadership as effectively guiding your staff to accomplish the goals and the mission of the company. To start this process, you must clearly understand what your leadership needs you to do.

1. THE STRATEGIC OFFICE

Embrace the vision and plans from the Strategic Office.

Your home office will be putting out a lot of guidance, instructions policy and information. You need to invest the time to gather this information. Then digest the information. Use the tools available to you to translate that into action.

Many times the Strategic Office will not package all the material you need in a nice easy to read letter and mail it off. You need to gather it and bring it together for your use. You can package it in a single letter and send it to your subordinates.

A lot of the information you need comes to you in the form of company newsletters, weekly bulletins, email snippets or conference calls. If you are a publically traded company, the Strategic Office will be required to publish forecasts. They will have press releases indicating their strategic plans. Their annual shareholders meeting will produce a lot of good information.

Most of the direction coming out will be good. Look at it. Your job is to support them. Be a leader and think about how to best implement the action on the Tactical Level. Ask what it is they are really trying to accomplish and get it done. Your job description is not to editorialize and place your disapproval stamp on the policy.

4. YOUR BOSS

The person that signs off on your paycheck. You are employed to perform work for your boss.

Once you have digested what your Strategic Office desires, have regular discussions with your boss to discuss it. Find out how your boss wants to implement the actions.

You boss will most likely have ideas of their own to try out or have some creative visions to bring to the front. Write it down. Take notes.

MET 2: Staff

Cleaning And Doing What Your Boss Asks

There are many jobs out there with lots of workers and bosses. Over the course of time, many workers have gotten into trouble for a wide range of reasons.

But there are two actions generally do not result in disciplinary actions.

First is cleaning. Employees who clean their areas and tidy the place up before leaving work are often able to do so without any form of disciplinary action.

Second is doing what your boss asks. People do not get into trouble for doing what the boss asks unless it is immoral, illegal, unethical, or if someone is going to get hurt.

If your boss asks you to do something, GO DO IT. Come to a stopping point and go do it.

Answer emails right away - even if it is just to acknowledge receipt. Make sure you follow up.

Meet all suspense's your boss or Strategic Office has for you. Many people blow off suspense's and the requestor has to chase them down. Do not get that reputation.

Support your leadership.

3. TRANSLATE THEIR DIRECTIONS INTO ACTION

Once you have digested the directions being given by the Strategic Office and your boss, you need to translate that into action. Formally, much of this will be used working Mission Essential Task 1, Objectives, Action Plans and Battle Rhythm.

Some of it will be passed informally through conversation and emails.

> **Translating the guidance from your Strategic Office into action is the cornerstone of leadership.**

Building a staff is useless if you do not send them off in a direction that supports your Strategic Office. Managing the flow of merchandise into your store in a way that is counter to the goals of your Strategic Office is poor leadership.

This translation is where a leader is made!

4. PROVIDE VALUABLE FEEDBACK

On the Operational Level, you are the connection between the Strategic and Tactical Level. Feedback is one of the most important things you can do for the Strategic Office. We just discussed your responsibilities in receiving their messages. You also have a responsibility to provide them feedback.

But don't shoot from the hip. Write it down. Make a coherent statement. Few things will make you look more stupid than giving half-assed feedback comments to your leadership. Few things will make you look smarter than when you are providing coherent and important feedback to your leadership.

Feedback on Successes: After completing a task, provide your boss with the feedback if there was a success. If you have developed a good working relationship with the department that initiated the task, go ahead and provide feedback directly to them.

It is easy to provide feedback on success. Everyone loves to hear how they produced success.

Feedback on Failures: But sometimes there is a failure. Often, a single task will produce a success and a failure. Your Strategic Office needs to get feedback if they produce something that failed. You need to send that feedback tactfully but clearly. State what you believed the intended outcome was and what the actual outcome was. Be clear about a constructive change you see as the solution for future events.

DO NOT just bitch about a failure. Do not go to your subordinates and point out how messed up the Strategic Office is. You can, and you should, go to your subordinates to solicit advice on how to make improvements. But do it in a way that is supportive and not detrimental.

Feedback on Opportunities: Sometimes, in the course of doing your business, you spot an opportunity. You need to present those opportunities to your leadership. Do not just do this off the cuff. Write out what the opportunity is, how to get it done and what benefit the company will get out of it.

MET 2: Staff

Part II The Staff You Lead

1. SELECT YOUR STAFF

Once you have digested the guidance and direction from your leadership, translated that into Action Plans, you need to get your staff on board to meet those Objectives.

The first step in leading your staff is through the recruitment and interview process. Selecting the right person for the job. It is a rare occasion that you are able to form a team from the ground up. Most of the time you will be joining a staff that is already in place. The advantages of having a staff already in place: They are familiar with the operation and can be functional while you get up to speed. Disadvantage: There may be some there that need to be weeded out, but have been there so long it becomes difficult, or impossible, to remove them. Also, bad or ineffective habits could be a way of doing business.

Soon enough, you will need to hire someone on your staff. You need to recruit and hire someone who is a fit for your store. You need to make sure your store is a fit for them. If you select a good candidate but your store is not a good fit for them; they will quit and you are back at the start. Take the time to go through a few candidates to get the right fit for both of you.

Where to Recruit

When looking for good candidates to hire, you can place a sign in the window and throw out an ad online - and you will need to do that. You will get better results by going out to seek candidates from potential pools.

If you follow Mission Essential Task 4 Community, you should have a binder that tells you all about your community. Use the information in the binder to recruit candidates.

Find your local schools. The colleges and high schools have young people looking for part time jobs. Go to the schools and talk to the guidance counselors or student unions. Tell them what you are looking for. This pool of candidates is primed to fill your schedule on the nights and weekends.

Next, look at any adult communities in the area. Go talk to the Home Owners Association (HOA). Request permission to attend one of their meetings to make a pitch. Place a small ad in their newsletter. Post a flyer in their community room. These fine people are prime candidates for your weekday hours. You can do almost the same drill for any community in your area.

Racism

The recruitment of candidates crosses over and intersects with Ethics.

You never want to limit the field you draw your candidates from.

In other words - racism, sexism, marginalizing groups, automatically discounting classes of people will limit the talent you bring in. Besides being immoral and illegal, it is just bad for business.

There was a guy named Glenn. Glenn laughed and said when he went to the temp agencies, he would give them a code word which meant no African Americans. It was sad that he did that and sad that the agencies supported it.

Don't be like Glenn.

As a leader - do not tolerate anyone who mimics Glenn.

Look for candidates across a broad spectrum. Make your selection based on skills needed for the job.

Base your candidate selection only on traits and characteristics that have a bearing on the job

---

Look at what organizations in your area that can provide resources.

The resources at the ARC. This group advocates and works with people with intellectual and developmental disabilities.

The ARC is a fantastic resource for your store. If during a busy season, you hire a bunch of temps from a regular agency to come in and clean, you will spend most of your day trying to find them and 3 seconds after you turn your back they loaf. Just the way it is.

When you hire a team or two from the ARC to come in, you win all around. They will have a group come in with a counselor. You explain to the counselor how to go through your store cleaning and straightening the shelves. You can go focus on other tasks. When you return it will be done. These folks love to work and are genuinely proud to do a good job. Cheap - minimum wage all around. The counselor is free. Buy them some pizza at the end of the shift (check with the counselor first). The employees will go home beaming with joy that they worked for you. They will beg their parents or guardians and counselors to come back. Something you will not get from a regular temp worker.

Also, you look good from a PR standpoint. More importantly - you increased your productivity, worked towards building your profits; and made some lives a whole lot better. You have become a better element for your community.

The Distributive Education Clubs of America (DECA) program has been a success for many businesses. This program for high school and college students. Team up with them to have a few students a year.

Bottom Line: Get to know the organizations in your community that are a resource for staff recruitment.

Position Standards & Application Review

Before you review the applications, write down the qualifications you are looking for. A cashier, a receiving dock worker, evening and weekend coverage, etc. Review your qualifications with your HR representative; do not do this in a vacuum.

In most cases, the applications are managed by HR and are completed online. You should have discussions with your HR for the qualifications you want listed on the recruiting website. You must shape the process at the start.

If you do not have an online process, make a list of **required qualifications**. This is a list of critical skills required to do the job.

Make a list of **desired qualifications**. This is a list of preferred skills, but the lack of one of these does not necessarily disqualify someone from the selection process.

The best method would be to have a check sheet to score each applicant against the job they applied for. This will ensure clear communication with your staff member screening the applications. The check sheet sets the stage where all applications are collected and reviewed with equal standards. This allows the staff member to review them faster, maintains the standards and allows to clear communication to anyone else checking.

Put the rejected applications in a file with a note specifying why the candidate was not referred to an interview. This will assist you in checking yourself as to why you are making a decision. When screening candidates, you need to ensure you are only disqualifying someone based on specific job qualifications. There are times when you need to limit the number of candidates referred to the next step. This leads you to placing candidates in the reject file that are otherwise qualified to continue. In this case, clearly note the application as a possible future interview.

For the candidates referred to an interview, use the selection checklist to rank the applicants. This just gives a good point of reference for the interviews.

Review the applications and line them up in order of preference. Make the calls to set up the interviews.

The Interview

The interview is the real place to set expectations for both sides. Be frank and upfront on what the job entails. Sell the good points about your store. Highlight that things about the job that are not so great.

Your employees will discover the unpleasantries of the job soon enough. You will be surprised at how well people accept doing the crappy things at work if they are told about it up front.

A store in Buffalo, NY was having a problem with high turnover in the first 90 days. If someone stayed longer than 90 days, they were there for a few years. The management team reviewed the problem to find out why this was happening.

The employees left because they were being asked to perform tasks beyond the scope of what they expected. A cashier was being tasked to change light bulbs and assist in unloading a truck. Their expectations did not match the job so they left.

Those that did not mind the extra work stayed. It was otherwise a good place to work.

The management team changed the interview script to address the concern. At the conclusion of the interview, if it seemed likely the candidate would be hired, the interviewer presented a list of the additional duties that went with the job. It was clearly stated to the candidate they would be changing light bulbs, unloading trucks and cleaning potties.

The result was a significant drop in the 90 day turnover rate. Most candidates were receptive to the additional duties during the interview. There were very few that balked at these other tasks.

The takeaway is that setting expectations during the recruitment and interview process will greatly reduce turnover.

What should you look for in an interview?

Have a standard set of questions for each position. Again, review this with your HR representative. Make sure you are following company standards and policies. This offers consistency. You will have different people conducting the interviews. It ensures that the interviewer is looking at what qualifications are needed for that position. Don't hire the world's best wide receiver to fill a linebacker's position.

Does the candidate have a good attitude?

You are hiring most people at minimum wage or slightly above. There are no highly technical positions in your store with salaries above $120,000.

You are not seeking a unique and highly polished set of skills from the candidate. In most cases they will be ringing a register or stocking shelves. If your candidate has a good attitude, you can work it from there. Hiring someone who is smart enough to design the space shuttle who runs around your store with a butt face because they hate life is not a win.

2. TRAIN YOUR STAFF

Training and developing your staff has two benefits.

   It produces a more knowledgeable staff.
When your staff is trained to your standards, they will be off to doing great things.

   It can give the staff a feeling of being important.
One of the worse feelings is being given a job you are unfamiliar with and told to just go do it. You feel like you are thrown to the wolves. When you train your staff, you are communicating to them your desire to see them succeed.

There are 4 types of training in retail:

> ### 1. Initial Training (read the ethics card and sign here)

On the first day, most stores will have employees go through the orientation training. This often consists of watching some videos, reading a few documents and signing a piece of paper that says they read the employee handbook. Many times, this actually involves the instructor asking everyone to rip out the last page and sign it while telling the group to read it later on their own time. It is tough to make orientation training exciting or even mildly entertaining. But it is necessary to get through this.

NOTE - As a leader, it is important that you incorporate the values of the introductory training into the daily activities of the store. This will give it emphasis and more meaning. You are the agent that takes the Strategic Office's guidance and puts it into action. This is their guidance. You should sit through it once a year. If it seems painful, maybe you should do something to make it better.

> ### 2. Training on the basic functions of the store (cashier training)

The training that shows the employee how to do the basic functions of the job. The purpose is to teach the employees the mechanics of operating a retail store. These center around properly accounting for the money and merchandise, safety, and merchandising display standards.

- Ring on the registers
- Receive a truck
- Operating a forklift
- Printing signs

➢ 3. Product training

The purpose for product training is to increase sales. A natural byproduct of this training will be reduced return rates. Focus your product training on how the customer will use the item and add-on sales that will enhance their experience. Mission Essential Task 5 Stock, has more about product training.

➢ 4. Development training

Development training is focused on building an employee's skills for a long term gain. Most development training is structured in a series of increasing levels of difficulty. Not all employees will be candidates for development training. Chose the ones with the most potential to excel for this training.

Sales Training

The most basic development training in the retail industry is sales training. This often starts with the basics of customer interactions and builds up to selling higher ticket items with add-ons.

Sales training is not a product offering from Griffin Gorge. There are many great companies that offer this service. You should shop around to find one that can service your store. You will get a high return on investment to have a company conduct one or two training sessions a year for some of your key sales team. A District Manager should combine the training for several stores. Depending on the type of store you have, send a strong employee to higher level sales training.

Computer Skills Training

If you have employees working a large part of their day on computers using Excel, Word, or Outlook, you need to send them to additional training. While someone may be literate on these programs, there are a lot of ways to improve your productivity in their use. The time and money spent will often be gained back by the increased productivity.

Cross Pollination

A very productive development training event is to send employees to another store to work. This can apply to managers, receiving, sales, cashier, and back office. By doing this, good habits are transferred across your organization. Bad habits fall away.

3. DIRECT YOUR STAFF

Mr. Rowinski & His Sockets

Mr Rowinski was once the manager of a large hardware store. He was very fond of giving direction. He rather enjoyed assembling a group of cashiers and stockers together to work on a project. These projects were often random in nature. One fine day he had a vision for a new way to display the sockets.

Now this store had every socket size possible. There were 6 point, 12 point and stars. Regular sockets and deep sockets. Metric and standard. Also an impressive array of specialty attachments, extensions and swivels. All available on 1/4, 3/8 or 1/2 inch drives.

Mr. Rowinski had six of his employees lined up, gave them his vision and put them to work moving these sockets. Each socket was on a single peg. He stood over them as they laboriously hacked away. This was not simple, as each socket peg coming down did not exactly have an empty space to be moved into.

As the day wore on, Mr. Rowinski kept coming by to check up on his masterpiece. The six employees ignored every customer. When lunch came, the project was completed. The proud six employees stood over their accomplishment. Mr. Rowinski carefully inspected the work. He folded his arms and stared one way then from another angle. He announced his verdict. It was terrific ---- However... It would look even better if all the pegs were moved 16 inches to the left.

The afternoon rolled to a close and the sockets had miraculously moved 16 inches after 12 hands bled. Mr. Rowinski once again inspected. He suggested it pegs get moved up a few inches so the box sets could fit better underneath.

Several days later, enough sockets were moved to appease Mr Rowinski. The socket sales for those few days were pretty pathetic.

Mr Rowinski engaged key resources for his store to conduct tasks that were counter-productive to sales. The employees were careful with the first move and with some pride, did a lot of extra little things to make it look good. The final move contained absolutely no extra effort and pride for the project left at the first coffee break.

Mr Rowinski was released from the company for his precipitous drop in sales. More to the problem - he was an intelligent person that was never trained. He had some good ideas but no concept on how to effectively turn that into action with his staff.

A well-directed staff will produce outstanding results for you and your company. It is amazing how most employees like being given clear directions, working hard to complete actions that are well thought out, and seeing positive results from their labor. It is a natural human reaction to have a feeling of satisfaction after completing some meaningful work.

Actions Plans

Action Plans are designed as a mechanism for a leader to carefully manage the store resources (staff) and direct them to an Objective. When your staff sees you doing this, you will see the results shine with their pride. It leads them to taking ownership in your business. They also will know why they are doing something developing ownership in the end result.

Scheduling

If you can do anything in your planning, foresight and great leadership - here it is. Piss poor scheduling is among the biggest reasons for turnover in a retail store. You need to make the schedule steady and make it early.

Some companies have gone to having a computer program generate the schedule. This is the Strategic Office's way of micromanaging a problem that is on the Operational Level. Their efforts would be better invested training their Operational leaders.

Scheduling is a bit of an art. It is NOT something that can be solved with a computer application. With some planning and investment of your time, a good schedule will be solving a host of secondary problems.

First - a store that is well set up can effectively run with a minimal staff during a rush. You don't need to match the number of employees on the floor with the customers.

You stock shelves more efficiently when the store is closed. You should conduct training or floor moves during slow times.

When your rush comes, if the shelves are stocked, the floor is neat, the signs are up, the displays are pretty, the registers are full of bags and register tape; you don't need a lot of employees on the clock.

> **YOU NEED TO SCHEDULE EMPLOYEES TO MATCH THE WORK**
> **-**
> **NOT THE SALES**

MET 2: Staff

Let's look at what you can do to make a good schedule.

First - *get a good list of availability from each employee*. Know how many hours per week they are available.

Work with the students on when they will need time for finals and other big projects. Your students will be cutting you out to make their finals. A student that blows off finals to work a minimum wage job is probably not the brightest bulb in the tool box. You can work with them to plan it or jump through hoops at the last minute.

Second look at your **Action Plans and Battle Rhythm.** What are some things you need accomplished each week?

    When are your trucks scheduled?
    When do you want displays changed?
    When do you want a focused clean up in an area?
    What are your anticipated sales?

Now start matching your staff to your Action Plans. When you put someone on your schedule at a time you want them to be changing displays - note it. Communicate how the schedule is supporting your plan.

Third, **be consistent.** Give the full timers the same day off during the week.

If a part time worker says they are available three afternoons a week. Schedule them for the same three afternoons every week. It will make it easier for both of you. If you start switching their days around - at the last hour - she will be switching jobs - at the last hour. Worse, they will be coming in and not caring how well your business is doing.

Forth, **publish the schedule early**. Tentatively schedule one month out lock it in two weeks out. This will help reduce turbulence for your employees.

If you are a Distract Manager, make sure you are working with your Store Managers on keeping a schedule that is a month out. Imagine the simple joy your employees might have if you did this for them. Don't be the leader that publishes the schedule the night before. Don't allow your Store Managers to lead like that.

Fifth, **build in some flexibility**. Kids get sick without giving you a month notice. You need to work with the young parents so they can take proper care of their family and still be productive employees. If you can support them, you will get their loyalty in return.

When there are family emergencies, you must support your employees. This is also where you may have some employees take advantage of your good nature. An employee lying about a family emergency to get time off should be dealt with as swiftly and forcefully as an employee who steals, fights or sexually harasses.

4. DEVELOP YOUR STAFF

Performance Plans & Reviews

Making proper use of the performance review process will set you above all others.

In many places, not just retail, the performance review process sucks. It is a pain in the ass drill that the human resource office makes you do once a year. They will have to ask twice before you make your first move.

Do your staff and your business a big favor - take control of the performance plan process. Don't just try to stay on top of it - use it to run your business into a profit.

Start with establishing a **performance plan**. Formally write out what you want the employee to accomplish over the next year. Use some of the same things you built off of your Action Plans. Spell out what they need to do to Meet Standards, Excellent or be Outstanding. Put in a metric for each level. Get input from the employee. Make this two parts. First from the position description you have for the job. Second, note where you have this person working on your Action Plans.

Take Wendy for example. She is listed as the primary point of contact for your Objective Frames.

> Meets Standards - Conducts all assignments listed in the Frame Action Plans.
>
> Excellent - Meets all metrics listed in the Frames Action Plan
>
> Outstanding - Coaches other stores on how to build an Action Plan for Frames.

Sometimes you can sit a group of cashiers down and review the standards for all the cashiers. This may be a good way to get some valuable feedback. But then finish it with a one on one with each.

You have established a base for performance. You have made clear expectations with measurables for what they need to do. You have listened to your employees for what they would like to accomplish in the next year. Reviews can be supplemented by positive counseling statements in writing. Six months is a long time to remember the good things that employees accomplish.

Then conduct an **interim review** - individually. These should be done at least once every six months; no need to be more than quarterly unless you are having a performance problem. The interim review should be formally recorded. Note where the employee stands currently and what might be expected in the next six months before the final evaluation. Make sure you solicit feedback from the employee. This is not a one way conversation.

Conduct a **final review**. This is the one that normally establishes what raise they get. If an employee walks in the review and gets something they did not expect, you failed. If you have clearly established the standards and conducted a good interim review, the final review should hold no surprises. Maybe make some good surprises for the outstanding employees.

Then start the process over for the next year. Three times a year at a minimum for each employee you supervise. Enforce this standard on the supervisors that report to you.

There was a fine gentleman named John A.

John A. had all these motivational leadership posters around his office. He often pontificated about how cultivating leaders was one of his core values.

John A. never sat down with his subordinates to discus performance standards. He never provided anything beyond a snippet in the hallway regarding their performance. He would email someone an evaluation to sign six to eight months after the due date. Most likely someone else provided the comments because he was too busy with important matters.

He was a well-trained leader that never put his training into action.

John A. was not a bad leader. You cannot be bad at something you don't do.

Coaching

You will need to direct your staff through coaching.

Think about a top notch basketball team. When a high performer comes off the court to the bench for a rest, a bad coach pats him on the back and says, "Good Job". A good coach points out the specific plays he did well in. The good coach tells him about a weakness in his opponent. He tells the player what to watch out for when he gets back in the game.

A good coach is pointing out the ways his staff can capitalize on their talents to increase the business. He shapes their actions through observation and encouragement.

While a good coach will occasionally resort to criticism, this should not be a normal way to communicate. People respond much better when you offer ways of improvement through positive actions. Reserve the criticism to events where it is really necessary.

You will have subordinate leaders. These are store managers, department managers, and floor leads. Then there are salespeople who are natural leaders. Know who they are.

> ### John at Lawrenceville
>
> John worked part time nights and weekends at a busy store in Lawrenceville, NJ. During the day he fixed trucks for the transportation department. Every night, John walked into the store like he owned it. Stopping by on his days off to see how everything was going. He directed the staff on daily activities. Telling people to go collect carts, take out the trash, clean the restrooms, stock shelves, etc.
>
> Often, John was often mistaken as the Store Manager. The real Store Manager, Connie and the District Manager Sheila took advice from John.
>
> John was a natural leader. Many studies have been conducted seeking to find if leaders are born or made. John never had any type of leadership training. He just cared about the place and had a desire for the store to succeed.
>
> The important lesson is how Connie and Sheila fostered the situation. John demonstrated his skills. His leadership supported him.
>
> Find the natural leaders in your store and foster their desire to lead. These leaders, like John, just might be part time. Give them the room to grow. Give them the encouragement. Reward them.

When you have an employee who "takes ownership" in your company good things follow. They will put in the extra effort. They will look out for your interests. They will support you when you need them. They will encourage the other staff.

Work to train and develop your emerging leaders. Give them standards and hold them to those standards. Always be more demanding (and rewarding) to those who are moving up. Find those that are rising stars and cultivate them.

In a field that is not known for high wages, you need to cultivate talent with the tools available.

Be careful to avoid the appearance favoritisms. There was a place we worked with that the CEO would go running in the morning with a select group. Those in his running club received the choice assignments and promotions. The general feeling in the company was that you had to belong to the running club to get those assignments. The CEO could very well have been choosing his top performers and invited them to go running. But the perception he created became the reality for many.

Listen.

Just listening to them. Many times your staff will have good ideas. Let them work those ideas. Allowing your staff to work their ideas is an active way of listening. Allow them to fail and learn. Do not punish honest failure, use it as a teaching moment.

5. REWARD YOUR STAFF

Compensation is what the worker gets for coming to work. Pay is usually at the top.

Work with your supervisor and Human Resources to get the best raises for your top performers. Rewarding outstanding employees is good business sense. It fosters a good work environment. In the long run you will find it attracts good talent.

Find if there is a way your company can give out small bonuses for exceptional work. A $100 - $200 cash bonus is awesome. A one shot deal that will mean a lot. If you selectively give a top performer a $200 bonus out of the blue - you can be guaranteed to get twice that back in their work performance.

Look at what else you can do for your employees.

Another form of compensation is moral boosting activities inside and outside of work. Sunday breakfast / cookout. Make a store bowling team. Help foster a family attitude.

Having good employees who like to work for your company will make your business better. Get a reputation as a great place to work. You will attract the talent.

Your customers can go to the competition; your employees can too.

6. COLLABORATE WITH PEERS

Build informal relationships with your peers.

As you move along in life, your peers are competitors to promotions, future bosses and future subordinates. You may remain peers as you move up together through the ranks.

Always Support Your Peers.

Only make good remarks about them to your boss and the leadership. Don't be the pot stirrer. You want word to get around that you treat people well. That is a good reputation to have. Do not work to undercut your closest competitor to the next promotion. People will see through it.

Remember – the theme for long term success lies with doing the right thing.

Actively Work To Collaborate With Your Peers.

Often they can help clarify issues, offer solutions to problems. Seek out their talents and learn from them. If one of your peers asks for your assistance, be there for them. Get ideas from them on building performance plans, making Objectives, tips on dealing with a difficult employee.

As we covered earlier about the personalities in a deck of cards. Seek to build off the strengths of your peers in areas you have a weakness.

You peers can often assist with resources when you need them.

Looking at this from the top down – A company that has strong peer groups that support each other will have long term success.

As a leader, support strong peer relationships amongst your subordinates.

7. CONCLUSION

Your staff is the most important element for you to manage. It is through them that you will accomplish your goals.

Be a good follower. Support your company leadership. Translate their desires into action.
Be a leader. Provide them with guidance and support that will meet your goals.
Be a great peer.

Mission Essential Task 3
Customer Service

1. INTRODUCTION

To provide the customers with a level of service that fosters a long term relationship that benefits both parties. In the retail business, selling merchandise to a customer is the sole source of income. The growth of the company comes from repeat business of a single customer and expanding the customer base to bring in new customers. Such growth requires a deliberate effort to enhance the customer's shopping experience. This MET centers on enhancement of the customer relationship through multiple lines of effort to include your staff, the product itself and shaping the customers perception of your company.

What is customer service?

Customer service means very different things to the CEO on the Strategic Level, you on the Operational Level, and the salesman on the Tactical Level.

The **Strategic Level** needs to set policies that guide the organization.

On the **Operational Level** you give guidance, enforce standards, and provide resources to the Tactical Level staff to implement policies from the Strategic Office.

On a **Tactical Level**, the salesman and cashiers need to be interacting directly with the customer to serve them.

Why Do You Need To Be Concerned With Customer Service?

Before we delve into the WHAT - you need to know the WHY. WHY do you even need to be concerned about customer service? Delivering customer service costs money.

In Mission Essential Task 9 Loss Prevention, we discuss that anything that takes your money and does not offer a return is a loss. Customer service costs money - but in your business it is money invested - not lost. In retail, you have a strong need for your business to invest in customer service. There are companies out there that do not need to make the investment.

Comcast Sucks (and they should) [3-1 to 3-6]

Comcast sucks at customer service. Almost any survey for customer satisfaction over the past few years has Comcast in the ten worst companies - ever. Hell, you would really have to try if you set out to be lower. Frontier Communications is trying like an SOB to catch up, but they have a little bit to go.

Why does Comcast fail at customer service? Because they have no need to make that investment. It does not make any business sense for Comcast to invest in customer service. They have no competition. Their customers are not going anywhere else.

Comcast would be doing a disservice to their stockholders if they invested in customer service. It costs money to answer the phone on the first ring, or the tenth ring or without having your customers wait on hold for 20 minutes.

It costs money to coordinate technician arrival times with customer availability. It's hard to have an intelligent human make that coordination. It's easier to use a computer that does not take into account some of the real problems in the world. It costs money to be nice - you will need to train and supervise your employees. Comcast stays in business and remains profitable because their customers have no other choice.

You, on the other hand, do not have that luxury. Your customers can find any product in your store somewhere else nearby or online. That's the WHY. Because you have competition and Comcast doesn't.

What Is Customer Service And What Does It Mean To You?

Task: Invest in customer service.

Purpose: To get the customer to give up their money and feel good about it.

Customer service is an investment. Your TASK is to invest time, money and resources into providing a service to your customers. It's about making it easier for them to spend their money.

Comcast customers have to give up their money. They have to get the service but Comcast does not need their customers to feel good about it.

Customers coming into your store are only going to give you their money if they feel good about it. You need to make them feel good about coughing up a piece of their paycheck.

You MUST invest in customer service to stay alive.

What can you do, on an Operational Level, to manage your company's investment into customer service?

2. SEVEN STEPS TO RETAIL CUSTOMER SERVICE

The first 3 are so important they are Mission Essential Tasks unto themselves.

A. Your Staff

Your staff is where you make your money in customer service. In Mission Essential Task 2 Staff, we cover a lot about hiring, training and mentoring your staff.

MET 3: Customer Service

How does your staff tie into customer service? Hiring, training and cultivating a staff that has a *good attitude* can - will - set your store apart.

YOUR JOB is to give your staff the resources they need to provide a high level of customer service.

"Smile or I will fire you," does not work for the long run. When you are treating your staff well, rewarding the performers and weeding out the undesirables, your customers will notice.

How many times have you walked through a store and noticed the employees have that have that look of just hating to be there. A sour face staff that only smiles when they clock out, hurts the bottom line.

Tasking your employees to finish something on the selling floor during open hours can be counterproductive to customer service. They become more concerned with finishing the task than with assisting a customer in parting with their money.

Chip ordered a part for his truck. After all, a Silverado likes to have its parts replaced.

Chip walked up to the parts desk. Behind the desk was the parts stockroom. A guy was working back there with a pissed off look on his face. When he saw Chip, he said, "These damn customers keep coming in and I can't get any work done." Chip paid for his part and told the clerk he would never bother him again. The parts clerk did not care in the least.

The real problem behind that counter was his leadership. They directed him to complete the stocking tasks, did not properly budget his time and most likely had some type of consequence for him if he did not finish stocking. The employee certainly did not benefit from providing customer service.

You need to properly resource your staff to provide a high level of customer service

B. Your Selling Floor

This is Mission Essential Task 7 (Note how these Mission Essential Tasks overlap at points).

Your selling floor is the crown jewel of your business. It is where the customer comes to interact with your business. The selling floor is where the customer hands over the cash.

A well-presented selling floor is customer service.

When a customer finds your presentation of the merchandise interesting and exciting, they will feel good about handing over their money.

A well merchandised selling floor will make or break the shopping experience for the customer. You will knock the socks off your competition if you ace this puppy.

C. Merchandise - Your Product Mix

In the chapter for Mission Essential Task 5 Merchandise, we go into more detail.

This may be one of the more difficult things for you to control on an Operational Level. Ask the question - Do you have the right product mix in your store?

A lot of this is set by the Strategic Office - but on the Operational Level you have some significant influence on events.

If you sell hammers - do you have nails? Sears once advertised themselves as "America's Hardware Store". They sold hammers but no nails; you had to go to a hardware store for those. Their buyers were lost on the irony of the situation.

Look at the main items you sell. Do you have the ancillary items that would go with it?

This is customer service. Can the customer go into your store to buy all the items needed for a project, or do they have to go shopping at several stores around town?

Need to pour a bag of concrete? Do you have all the tools and material in your store to do a concrete project?

Listen to your customers. If you get repeated requests for an item - maybe you should carry that item. Customers are walking into your store expecting that you will be carrying that item. Might be a good business choice to accommodate them before you get a reputation of not having everything needed for a project.

Communicate this with your home office. Often, your buyers might not realize a potential market.

D. Front End Management

A customer will spend an hour wandering around your store, looking at stuff, checking Facebook on their cell phone and texting to their friends.

But when it comes time to leave - they want to make a bee line to the register and get out of there. They want to pay and get out. No customer wants to wait in a big line so they have the opportunity to talk to the person in front of them.

When a customer comes up to give you their money - make it easy for them. Take their money - THAT IS WHAT YOU ARE THERE FOR !!!

So make it a point to take it from them quickly before they change their mind. Start with having clearly marked registers. Have some impulse items around, but it is counter-productive if they hide the registers.

You need to have a front end that runs smoothly - for your customer. Make sure the front end is stocked with the supplies needed to operate. Not good to run out of bags, register tape or change when you have a line.

Are the registers set up for the cashiers to be efficient (ask them)?

On a busy day observe your traffic flow patterns. See what you can do to manage the flow of traffic so people move efficiently. Customers have problems following signs. Manage the traffic flows through the placement of displays.

Line Management

Line management is something that needs attention every five minutes your store is open. The psychology of standing in a moving or not moving line has an effect on how your customer feels about their shopping experience.

A customer walks up to a line ten deep but it is moving along they will feel like you are efficient. Right next to that is a line two deep that is not moving fast and they feel like you are inefficient. The customers at the end of each line will leave at the same time with different feelings about your line management.

Get your cashiers to work as a team in line management. Train cashiers to spot problem lines and react. Do not allow one to shout "I'll take the next customer over here!" That is a sure way to cause fights and raise anxiety levels. Teach them to walk the customer over, "Sir, I'll ring you up over here."

Set the front end up to allow a good visual range over the registers. You will fail at line management of you are unable to even observe that there is a problem.

An effective, last resort, trick is to give the cashiers a few coupons to hand out to customers who wait too long in a line. This is a sure to change their attitude in a good way.

Pleasant Cashiers Will Increase Your Revenue

When the customers give you their hard earned money, the final action your company should complete is to be pleasant.

It's simple to understand that the cashier needs to greet the customer. Avoid having a pre-scripted line. Let the cashiers be themselves. If your Strategic Office allows, avoid pitching credit cards, bonus programs and other items. Most customers (and cashiers) find that annoying. Small talk coupled with a good farewell salutation makes for a pleasant transaction.

As the Operational manager, you must foster this.

- Move your staff around to have the more pleasant ones on the registers.
- Give appropriate breaks to allow them to refresh.
- Always give a break after a nasty customer.
- Allow a soda or water.

Even the most pleasant cashier is not pleasant everyday. Life will sometimes interfere. If a cashier is coming on shift after a rough day, assign them to some backroom work if they need an hour or so to adjust. Your cashiers, as a group, are the most important people in the entire company. They are the face of your organization.

If all of the cashiers walked off the job, in five minutes the Store Managers would be ringing the registers. If all the Store Managers walked off the job, the cashiers would stay on the registers.

E. Returns (3-7 to 3-12)

Returns are an opportunity for your business to grow.

Sure - returns hurt your profit in the short run. *To Sell Merchandise At A Profit* means you give the customer merchandise and they give you money.

When a customer comes in with a return you are going backwards. You are paying a cashier to give money back. All of us would much prefer to pay a cashier to take a customer's money. For returns, you are giving away money and getting back a piece of merchandise you probably don't want. It might be damaged or at a minimum it will have to be checked and repackaged.

Returns can grow your business in the long run.

MET 3: Customer Service

Short Term Loss -- Long Term Gain

In the short run, you lose the sale. You lose the money.

In retail we are here for the long game. You are building your business. Handling returns the right way will allow you to develop a more loyal customer base. Your local reputation grows in a positive way.

Rudy

Rudy worked as a department manager in a large box store in Freehold, NJ. She was tough on returns. At the end of the month, her department consistently showed the lowest return rate in the region. Her backend was empty in the Return To Vendor (RTV) bin.

When a cashier had a return, they had to leave the register and go find Rudy. The trick was to step away from the customer. Rudy would get the short story and tell the cashier to, "Make them work for it." The cashier had to go back and deny the return a few times. Many times the customer would leave without completing the return. Rudy would comment, "They really aren't mad. The sap will be in here next week to buy more anyway."

Not a good way to run a business and her sales eventually proved that.

The P&L at the end of the month started showing Rudy's sales lagging behind the rest of the store and region. Rudy was baffled.

When a customer comes in and wants to return a product, don't give them a hassle. Gladly give them a refund. More often than not, they will go back around in your store and shop to spend more money. Lowes has a special return entrance. Stand back and watch how many customers walk in to return an item and go back in to the store. Observe the smile on the cashier. Now go look up how well Lowes financials are.

The attitude the store leadership has in processing customer returns often reflects their views on a lot of other areas around the store. Is the attitude to make the customer feel good about doing business with you or is it to squeeze the customer out of every penny you can get?

How many customers say Comcast offers a pleasant experience with refunds?

Griffin Gorge Associates
To Sell Merchandise At A Profit

Avoid Selling a Return

A great way to reduce your returns is avoid selling an item that is destined to be returned. A well trained staff can do this for you. Analyze your returns and list the reasons the customer did not keep it. Here are some common problems.

The customer --

- Buys a product that is not designed to do what they need.
- Does not buy all the accessories to make it a complete package.
- Not sure if they need 3 or 4. Buys 4 and returns 1 later.
- Buys a product designed for low use but uses every day.
- Misuses the product and it breaks.
- Their significant other says, "Are you kidding me?"
- The product is poor quality.

You can reduce these buy training your staff and through signage explaining the product features. More about this is discussed in Mission Essential Task 9 Loss Prevention.

F. Dealing With The Difficult Customer

Everybody reading this will have to agree. If you have been out on the selling floor for more than a week -- one of the greatest pleasures a retail worker could ever have is to have the ability to beat the crap out of some of the customers.

Some customers are so rude and disgusting you may feel a good ass whopping is in order. Do America a favor and knock some of those teeth out. But as humorous as it might be to talk about it, it's not going to happen. Something even Comcast refrains from. And I am sure their customers get pretty upset with them. There are some really nasty people in the world. A few of them will find a way into your store.

Some Folks Just Hate Being Alive and Will Not Die

As a young buck, Chip worked on a boat taking people fishing out in the ocean. A middle aged couple would come out every two weeks and they were just nasty. They were rude. They treated their fishing adventure like they were doing chores. Chip asked how their morning was and they complained about having to get up so early to make the trip. There were boats leaving every four hours; so they could very well have slept in and still made a trip.

As the season wore on, Chip finally asked them why they hated life. Or did they go to work on Monday morning singing songs of joy. Then on Friday start moaning that the dreaded weekend fishing trip was coming up all too soon.

This is the couple that walks into your store and pisses off your staff.

But you are not there to feel good about the customer - you are there to get the customer to feel good about you. You are the adult in the situation. If your kids are acting up you do not start acting up too. Your job is to make the customer feel good so they give you money; not to prove them wrong.

As a leader, when your staff has a difficult customer, step up to the plate and pull the customer aside. You get paid to handle the problems.

- This allows you to handle the problem quickly.
- Keeps the cashier moving the lines along.
- Cashier does not get stressed.
- You might just find a systemic problem.
- Keeps the noise away from other customers.

As best you can, always back up your staff. A major complaint from retail workers is when they inform the customer of the policy, the customer complains, the manager comes over and just gives it to them. This creates a bad cycle of events.

> **Work with your boss and the front end manager to create policy and procedures to allow the most favorable decisions for the customer to be made by the cashier at the register.**

When The Difficult Customer Really Is Right

Sometimes a customer has a right to be upset with your store. You have a lot going on. You have a large staff. If you run a busy store you will eventually do something that does not make a customer feel good about their purchase and you are at fault. Period. It is the natural course of events.

You should like it when a difficult customer comes in to complain. They are expressing their displeasure about your store. They are giving you the opportunity to improve it. They are standing in front of you and you have a chance to keep them as a customer. View the complaining customer as an opportunity to keep their business.

The ghost customer is bad. This is the customer that comes into your store un-noticed. They have a problem and leave upset. They tell no one. They just walk away. And never return. You have no chance to know what the problem was and no chance to fix it. Whatever upset them off is probably happening to other customers.

Griffin Gorge Associates
To Sell Merchandise At A Profit

Ted

Ted was a lazy, but smart, individual. He became a master at dealing with difficult customers because he was lazy.

Ted would step up to a complaining customer and simply ask, "What would you like me to do?" and then he did it. Often, what the customer asked for was less than what Ted was willing to do. In large part, Ted was just wanted to end the conversation as fast as he could. The customers were always pleased with the outcome. After all, they got just what they asked for.

When you have a complaining customer in front of you, just asking them what they want is a good start to fixing the problem.

Ken And His Flowers

Ken was a very unique person - in a good way. Ken was the guy you passed the irate customer to. He had a charm about him. A natural charming personality.

When someone had a difficult nasty customer, the rule was to pass them off to Ken.

Ken could handle any of them. One of his tricks was buying flowers. When a lady customer was upset, Ken would get her address and send her flowers from the store. He had a budget and an account set up with a local florist.

He noted that no matter how pissed and upset they were, it always turned them when he sent flowers. Think about it. She gets home and the flowers arrive. For a week they are sitting out for display in her home. Her friends and family see them. She has no choice but to say how well Ken fixed her problem.

On weeks when Ken had no irate customers, he just sent flowers out to someone anyway. Ken got his leadership to give him the budget. Ken made a lot of money for that store.

Ken and his Operational Leadership made the company invest in customer service. His business grew and that was not by accident.

Ever have a problem with Comcast and then find flowers at your doorstep the next day?

G. The Little Things

Listen To The Customer

Just like you need to listen to your staff - you need to listen to your customers. Your customers are more than willing to tell you the good and bad things about your store. If they like something in your store find a way to exploit it.

If they are telling you something negative about your store - work to fix it or mitigate it.

But the key here is to listen. How do you listen?

Walk your floor. Make it part of your Battle Rhythm. Stop and engage. You need some level of skill to know when a customer wants to talk and when they want you to stay out of their way. Don't force a conversation on those in a hurry.

A salesman on the Tactical Level will be seeking to engage the customer so he can sell more goods. On the Operational Level, you need to engage the customers to find way to improve your business. Almost the same conversation but you are sorting the data - the information - in a different way for different outcomes.

The Story Of Bob

Bob will teach you how to set your store apart from Amazon.

One of the greatest threats to a brick and mortar store is Amazon. Amazon is out there putting the brick and mortar stores out of business.

If you take lessons from Bob you can grow more stores.

Bob worked in a store that had a large electronics section. Anybody who is familiar with selling electronics will tell you this is a cut throat business with razor thin margins.

Bob was one of the best salesman in retail. He had customers coming in that would only deal with him. Drive all the way to the store "Bob's not here. That's ok - I'll come back later." Drive all the way home and come back later when Bob was on.

Why were customers coming back like that? Bob would listen to them and take notes. If a customer came in and bought a camcorder, he would write a little note. "Jim bought a camcorder model Q36 on Sunday. He wanted to film his little Suzie in a basketball game next Thursday."

Bob would call him up the next Saturday and say "Hi Jim. How did Suzie do in the game? Did she play well? How did the team do? Did you get some good shots with the camcorder?" The customer would naturally brag about his daughter. Then go into how the camcorder worked. If they guy did not understand something, Bob would help him out.

Ask the other salesmen if they ever called their customers. The general reaction was such an endeavor is a waste of time. Usually the customer has a complaint or it takes too much time away from sitting on the sales floor.

Did you ever get a call from the salesman at Amazon asking if you know all the buttons on your new camcorder? Ever have Comcast call to ask if you needed help programing your TV to get the best out of your cable service?

Bob made real connections to his customers. Bob made money. Be like Bob.

As a side note - Bob memorized every zip code and county road in New Jersey.

Terry at Eddie Bauer

Terry worked at a small store in the local mall. He dedicated one evening a week to sit at home and hand write thank you letters to his customers. A personalized note. He would drop a coupon in the envelope. Sometimes he used a postcard just to make it easier. Terry built a strong following for his store.

Bottom line here - interact with your customers. Allow your staff the time and small pocket change needed to put your business above the others.

Communication With The Customer

There are two ways a customer will reach out to find information about your store: through a telephone call or website.

Make sure the telephone in the store gets answered on the first few rings. Set up your team so that a customer is not waiting on hold for the right person to assist them. Answer the telephone ready to talk to the customer. Do not give the answering duties to someone who is too busy to converse with the customer. If your store has a recording machine that says, "press 1 for xx, 2 for yy", smash it.

Monitor your website. Put this on your Battle Rhythm for a monthly or quarterly check. The folks back at the home office managing the site will make changes without communicating with you.

Be A Part Of Your Community

This rolls right into being a part of the community. You perform a critical function for your community.

Customer interaction is the foundation to your retail brick and mortar stores. You must invest in building a strong foundation that will allow your store to endure.

On an Operational Level - train and support your floor staff to interact with the customers. Allow them to invest the time.

3. CONCLUSION

There are significant changes in the marketplace with the online competition that can affect your store. Brick and mortar stores have the benefits over online stores in customer service. Investing in Customer Service will cost you in the short term; in the long term it will ensure you are an enduring and profitable mission.

MISSION ESSENTIAL TASK 4
COMMUNITY

1. INTRODUCTION

To gain an understanding of the multiple layers of your community. Operating a retail store involves setting up a building in a community. This community is the source of your customers and your staff. Just like people, every community has a personality that makes it unique from any other community. Unlike people, communities often exist for hundreds of years. Some evolve to change over the course of a decade and other remain stable. This MET centers on the need for Operational Level leaders to understand their community in order to better serve them and to draw talent to staff their growing business.

A District Manager and Store Managers must invest the time to understand their community.

Task: Make a binder that contains information about your customer base and the community. Gain knowledge about your customers.

Purpose: To find ways to exploit your business to increase sales and better serve the community. Secondary effect is finding sources for employees.

This chapter is for a store already in operation. This is not about getting customer base information for opening a new store. While much of the same information may be collected, the way the data is sorted and used will be very different.

The Strategic Level marketing and buying teams will use much of the same information for their analysis for ongoing operations - but again that is sorting this information in a much different way.

The District and Store Managers can use this information to exploit ways to increase sales. Once you develop a good understanding of the customers coming in your door, the better you will find opportunities. These are the people coming in to give you their money. These are the people you seek to provide a high level of customer service. You need to understand them.

Make a binder and keep the following information. Most likely, you will start the binder and build it out over the course of a year. Update this and make notes.

2. THE BINDER

TAB 1 MAPS

➢ Start with a basic map of the state, or surrounding states. Then get county maps for the adjacent areas. Get a map that shows the zip codes in your area.

➢ Get a detailed town map and hang it on your wall.

- ✓ Mark the map with locations your customers are coming from.

- ✓ Mark the names of the key developments in your area. Add contact information for any homeowners associations (HOA).

- ✓ Mark the colloquial names for any of the areas.

TAB 2 DEMOGRAPHICS

Find the key towns or areas your customers are coming from. A great source for this information is at census.gov. This is a treasure trove of information that can be sorted in various ways. You can sort it by county, zip code and congressional district.

Download information gathered from the census and build a profile for each to include:

- Population Data by Age
- Income Ranges
- Education Levels
- Ethnicities

TAB 3 INDUSTRIES

Start this tab with the census data which will group employers by type.

Then go to the chamber of commerce to get a member listing. Conduct some research on these businesses. No need to write a thesis paper, just get some of the basic information.

TAB 4 INSTITUTIONS

Make a list of the following along with a short note on them.

- Local School Districts
- Colleges
- Universities
- Hospitals/Medical Centers
- Charities
- Community groups

TAB 5 TRANSPORTATION STRUCTURE

Draft some short notes on the transportation in the area specific to the following list. These will be on your maps, but you do need to get some short background notes.

Key Highways	Logistical nodes
Rail system	Public transit system

TAB 6 HISTORY

Draft a short history of the region you are in. Write how the population and economy evolved to where it is today. A local library just might your best source.

TAB 7 POLITICAL

Get a list of the elected officials in your area:

> Town Mayor
> Town Council
> County Officials
> State Government
> Federal Representatives

A key source of information for you will be the town mayor and some of the more local elected officials. These folks are in the business to know their constituents. You need to reach out to them and build a relationship. Invite them to visit your store. Take some out to lunch on a regular basis.

Use them to gather information. Their job is to know the community. They will be glad to fill you in. Some of them can breathe life into the information you collected in the other tabs. The elected officials can often give you some background as the "why" behind some of the cold facts you get off the census pages.

3. AFTER THE BINDER

The next few points are not in the binder - these are things you need to add to your Battle Rhythm.

Local Newspaper

Subscribe to a local newspaper. Read it each morning with a cup of coffee. Don't just read a few headlines. Read the notices for what community groups are meeting. How are the local high school sport teams doing? What major events are coming up?

Social Media

Follow your company guidelines for social media. Get on different review sites and bulletin boards that might talk about your store. Find out what is being said about you. If your company policy allows, respond in an adult way to the reviews; both the good and the bad. You can make a lot of good progress in responding to problems your customers may have.

If your company has a Facebook page or other social media, you need to get on and follow.

MET 4: Community

Town Meetings

Attend some of the town meetings when you can. Follow their website for any town news. This is where you may find changes that will affect your store.

On occasion, attend a school board meeting.

4. CONCLUSION

What does it accomplish to gather all this information? You are learning and understanding the people that shop in your store.

Walk into work knowing the events happening about town.

Thinking like Sun Tzu; you are finding ways to exploit your market.

Gather this information and you will start to see opportunities to sell.

You will find sources for good employees.

You will be ahead of your competition.

This is about gathering knowledge to help shape the future of your business.

MISSION ESSENTIAL TASK 5
MERCHANDISE

1. INTRODUCTION

To provide the customers with the merchandise tailored to your company theme and the needs of the customers. All parties should expect that the store staff has a knowledge of their merchandise. This MET centers on store having the correct mix to provide both a convenience for the customer and to increase sales. By virtue of being the seller, your staff is expected to maintain a proficient level of knowledge of the merchandise in order to support the needs of the customer.

This Mission Essential Task has two distinct sections.

- The correct product mix for your stores
- A trained staff to sell those products

In here, by extension, when we mention stock it can also refer to any services that you sell.

2. THE CORRECT PRODUCT MIX

Task: To have the correct product and services mix in your stores.

Purpose: To provide the customers with the goods and services they expect and need.

This may be one of the more difficult things for you to control on an Operational Level. Ask the question - Do you have the right product mix in your store?

We discussed this in Customer Service. Can the customer go into your store and buy all the items needed? Or do they have to go shopping at several stores around town? Look at the main items you sell. Do you have the ancillary items that would go with it?

Your store may sell an assortment of window dressings. Don't just look at the window dressings and think you have everything. Do a practical exercise. Walk into your store. Buy some window dressings. Go home and put them up. Use ONLY items purchased in YOUR store. See how it goes.

Update your list of what is needed each time you run back to your store or another store. Now you have a list of what to carry and put them all together.

Why carry all the ancillary items needed to put up window dressings? Because many of the customers for that item have just moved into a new home. They might not have everything they need to include a small level and screwdriver.

Listen to your customers. If you get repeated requests for an item - maybe you should carry that item. Customers are walking into your store expecting that you will be carrying that item. Might be a good business choice to accommodate them before you get a reputation of not having everything needed for a project.

Communicate this with your home office. Often, your buyers might not realize a potential market.

Story of Pink Flamingos

Working with a large retailer, we entered a new market by opening a store in Buffalo, NY. Set in the east side of the area in the town of Cheektowaga. This town has a heavy Polish immigrant population. For reasons unexplained in nature, the Polish community in Cheektowaga just loves anything to do with pink flamingos.

Lawn ornaments, shower curtains, toilet bowl brushes and napkin rings.

The company had a small inventory of these items and in most other stores the sales were lackluster. We sent word out to the other stores to send us their excess inventory.

We discussed this with the buyer, who was baffled as to why this was a quirk for Cheektowaga.

A small display of pink flamingo items in the front display window drew a fair amount of traffic into the store. The pink flamingo items sold fast and it created a lot of secondary sales.

This was a combination of listening, understanding the customer base and cooperation with the Strategic Office.

---

3. YOUR STAFF ARE THE PRODUCT EXPERTS

Task: To have a staff educated on the products and services.

Purpose: To increase the sales and reduce returns through staff interactions with the customers.

Focus your product training on how the customer will use the item and add-on sales that will enhance their experience.

You are the seller for the merchandise. Your customers expect you to be able to know how your products work. If you invest in product training, you will see increased customer satisfaction through higher sales.

The best source for product training will be the manufacturer. Many manufacturers have representatives that have a financial interest in you selling more of their products. Work through your buying office to arrange training. While this is a great investment, your time is limited. Seek product training at the start of a season and for items with high visibility or high profit margins.

Thorlo Socks

The Thorlo sock company sends representatives out to clothing stores to make a product training spiel. We are talking about simple socks. This is not some high tech gadget with buttons.

In fact, the idea of taking employees off the floor for sock product training seems almost comical. But Thorlo does it right. The training is less than 30 minutes. The representative is enthusiastic. We are baffled at how you can recruit a team that loves socks like they do.

The return on investment was there. The socks sell at a high price with a decent profit margin. Their sock sales increased significantly after the training.

The socks are also pretty damn good.

The Customer's View

Gear the training towards the customer point of view.

GoreTex once went around doing product training with some amusing results. The representative gave detailed scientific explanations on how GoreTex works and why it was absolutely necessary to own a GoreTex jacket if you were going to make it through life. Then the salesmen hit the floor, putting their new knowledge to the test. A customer walks in and the salesman pounces. "Hi. This jacket you are looking at is the greatest piece of outerwear you will ever invest in. The tri-laminated membrane is rated to be a semi permeable dual converted barrier to any form of dihydrogen monoxide. The characteristics of the microporous primary membranic layer will allow only a single directional transition flow of the vapor product traveling at an ambient saturation." A smile of self-satisfaction emerges at the ability to recite that in one breath.

A puzzled customer looks up and asks, "Will this keep me dry in a summer rain without sweating my balls off?"

"Yeah. Basically."

Don't overthink your customer.

Other Sources

Other training can come from your seasoned employees teaching the new ones. You need to draft an outline of points to cover and schedule a time for this. While it is beneficial to pair a seasoned employee with a new one for mentorship, you must plan and schedule key product training.

Or maybe - just maybe - a new kid on the block brings some knowledge to share with the seasoned employees.

A District Manager can consolidate product training between their stores; depending on distance.

Training videos or even YouTube demonstrations can be very helpful. Just be careful of the source. You should review these first and provide a list for your employees to watch. Allow them to do this on work time. Don't be a jerk and require, or even suggest, they watch these on break or at home. The purpose is to educate them on your products in an effort to increase your sales. If possible, record your own to give to customers or put on YouTube.

Training Will Get Results

A staff well trained in product knowledge can:

1. Make a sale by working with the customer.

2. Increase sales by getting the add-ons.

3. Increase the customer satisfaction by getting them a product with all the accessories to do the job.

4. Reduce returns by actually selling the customer the right product for the right job.

5. Please do not over sell to a customer just to make a target. This is a bad short term strategy.

On the Operational Level, your job is to provide the training to your staff.

MISSION ESSENTIAL TASK 6
INVENTORY MANAGEMENT

To manage the physical flow of the merchandise. The inventory you have in the store represents a significant investment on the part of the Strategic Office. This MET centers on maintaining proper accountability of the inventory, provides a mechanism to have situational awareness of your assets and to reduce loss. Once you are aware of your inventory on hand, monitoring sales and forecasting, you will be in a position to control the flow of inventory to match the needs of your business.

This Mission Essential Task has two parts:

1. Accountability of the merchandise

2. Managing the flow of the merchandise

Part I. Accountability Of The Merchandise

You are the person responsible for millions of dollars in merchandise. This is not a static set. You have a large volume coming in on the receiving dock, it goes on the shelves and then out the front door. You must manage the accounting of the merchandise in order to be aware of what to reorder and to reduce shrink. The Strategic Office hired you with the trust that you will properly account for their assets.

Task: To keep accurate accounting of the inventory for your store.

Purpose: To properly manage the volume of goods and reduce shrink.

Inventory management is a central element in keeping your profits in line.

- You need to know what you have in order for you to sell it and reorder it - SALES

- One of your keys to PROFIT is having a low shrink rate.

1. RECEIVING

Inventory management starts when the merchandise comes in on the receiving dock. As a leader you need to fully understand the process your company has to receive merchandise and then walk the area to enforce those standards.

Make it part of your daily Battle Rhythm to walk the receiving dock. Watch what is going on and engage your staff. Watch to make sure they are properly accounting for the merchandise.

A big issue is to make sure the area is clean and neat. Enforce the standard that the area is cleaned, swept, boxes lined up and equipment properly stored before the dock closes each day. It will have an impact on the way the staff treats the merchandise. People will take better care of everything when you enforce cleanliness standards.

Periodically, make unannounced visits to sit down with your receiving supervisor to review the paperwork. Check that they are properly following the company procedures and not taking short cuts.

Make daily rounds through the stock rooms. Assign individuals responsibility for each section. Provide them with the time and resources to keep the area up to standards.

2. FRONT END

Managing the front end plays into a lot of areas to include Inventory Management. Properly accounting for the merchandise leaving the store is critical in your accountability.

Just like the receiving dock, enforcing cleanliness standards makes a positive impact. On the Front End it effects Customer Service, Loss Prevention and Inventory Management.

Work with the front end supervisor to ensure the cashiers are properly scanning the merchandise. A common mistake is ringing multiple quantities. Train the cashiers to check all items; a stack of ten same looking items might actually be two SKUs.

Hopefully, your store has a system to track items improperly scanned. Make sure this report is checked. Find the source of the errors. Items could be marked wrong, loaded improperly in the system, cashier error or receiving error.

Talk to your cashiers about issues they have about the way things are managed at the front end. If you have frank discussions with them, you will be getting some good feedback in identifying problems with accounting for your merchandise.

The closeout procedures for your registers are normally established by your Strategic Office and are detailed for how the cash and receipts are processed. You need to be an expert on this process and spend some time each week reviewing it. Again, just your presence showing concern will be enough to keep the others doing it right.

3. RECORDS

The Strategic Office sets policy for how your audit records are kept. Assign someone to track these. Get specific on your expectations by putting them on the associates performance evaluation standards. This is a short paragraph, but do not under-estimate the importance of well-kept audit records.

4. INVENTORY DAY

Most stores will conduct a store wide inventory annually. This should be the most important single day of the year - and the most stressful. A good inventory will reset the counts for your inventory numbers while establishing your shrink number. A bad inventory will result in poor accounting and profit losses that will affect your store for years.

> One store we worked with seemed elated that their annual inventory numbers came back and showed absolutely no shrink. This was not a good indicator on our radar. Every store, through normal wear and tear, will have some shrink.
>
> We asked how the previous year shrink looked and they stated it was really bad at 4.0%. Upon a forensics review, we found (to no surprise) they missed inventorying an entire section last year.
>
> Their sales for that section were off kilter. The inventory counts got adjusted for the missing goods and more inventory was sent in. Excess inventory resulted in markdowns and reshipping costs to move it to other stores.
>
> The failure of that staff to properly inventory the store had a major negative impact on their profit.

You should really start the process six months before the date.

Use the backward planning method. Start with the inventory date, then start writing out what events need to be completed the day before, the week before, the month before, etc. Build a calendar showing the progress of events up to the inventory day.

Second, assign individuals or position to get each task completed. Give them the resources to complete the tasks.

Third, review the plan with your boss and key managers. Get their input and guidance.

Forth, disseminate the calendar and tasks to the staff. Let everyone see all the events; do not just give a person their part. By allowing everyone to see the entire plan, you show them how their actions influence others.

Fifth, conduct weekly checks that the plan is being followed. Make adjustments as needed. Use a store floor map to assist you in tracking the progress.

Sixth, after the inventory day make adjustments you would want for next year. Get feedback from everyone involved.

A great way to tackle this is to build out an Operations Plan and discussed in Mission Essential Task 10 Problem Solving. Skip the problem solving process and just go to the

MET 6: Inventory Management

part where you build the plan. Your Inventory Day Operations Plan (OPLAN) is a proven method to ensure a successful inventory. The OPLAN will coordinate the efforts of many people over the course of several months. It will be easy to share and easy to re-use each year. It builds off of the lessons learned.

Griffin Gorge offers a service to build an Inventory OPLAN for your stores. While a chain of stores may have a similar OPLAN, each store is so unique that it must have its own to be successful.

Measure your success when the final numbers come in to evaluate your success. The industry average for shrink in a retail store is about 1.4%. Your store should be near that target.

	This Year	Last Year	2 Years
Your Company shrink #:	_____	_____	_____
Your Regional shrink #:	_____	_____	_____
Your District shrink #:	_____	_____	_____
Your Store shrink #:	_____	_____	_____

Look at the trends here. Review this with your boss and key leaders. If there any anomalies you should take this through the full problem solving process and analyze the WHY.

Griffin Gorge Associates
To Sell Merchandise At A Profit

Part II. Managing The Flow Of The Merchandise

1. INTRODUCTION

Once you are properly accounting for the merchandise, you are able to start managing the flow of the goods to meet your sales.

We stated in the Introduction that you need to get a passing grade in each Mission Essential Task to win. In every store we have ever worked with - without exception - those Operational Leaders that mastered the flow of merchandise had the largest sales increases.

Strive to master your inventory flow and you will crush the sales. Many other things will work out if you let others run them. The goods will get from the truck to the floor. The registers will ring. The lights will come on. But managing the flow of merchandise takes a dedicated leader to work it.

Mastering the flow of merchandise is part science and part intuition.

This is where Operational Leaders will earn their paycheck!!

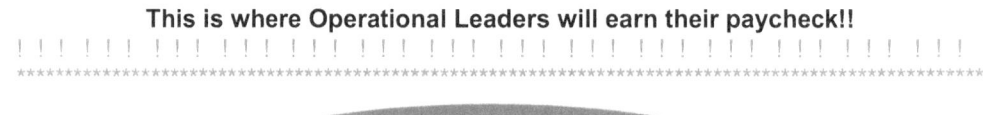

Managing and directing the flow of merchandise will drive your sales over the top.

Invest extra effort in this Mission Essential Task. Use this to train and mentor your key leaders.

2. MAP YOUR SECTION SALES

Your store should have a report that shows the inventory by item, dollar amount and section. Review this report on a monthly basis. If you have a large store, review a set of sections each week so that you cover the entire store each month. This can be a very good tool in managing the flow of merchandise.

In Mission Essential Task 7 Selling Floor, we discuss the need for mapping out the floor. Take a copy of this map and use it to manage the flow. Make a map for each quarter, or for each major seasonal change.

- Mark which areas have seasonal fluctuations. Write out what areas will expand or contract as the seasons ebb.

MET 6: Inventory Management

- Mark the LY sales increase/decrease for the areas. Make a note if you expect the same for TY or what difference you might expect.

- Discuss these maps with your boss and key leaders. You are seeking their opinion on the change in sales. At a later time you will review the product details to drive the changes.

- What new items are coming in that will affect sales? What past performers can you count on again? Write these down and get some feedback from other stores.

- Find out what items/sections the Strategic Office will be chasing.

3. PLAN FOR YOUR ORDERS

Now comes the tedious part.

	A	B	C	D	E	F	G	H	I	J	K
1	POWER TOOL SECTION		CURRENT	WEEK 1		WEEK 2		WEEK 3		WEEK 4	
2		SKU	OH	LY	TY	LY	TY	LY	TY	LY	TY
3	CORDLESS DRILLS	76789	117	65	81	77	96	86	107	95	119
4		3684	281	156	195	184	230	206	258	229	286
5		84555	49	27	34	32	40	36	45	40	50
6		9745	45	25	31	30	37	33	41	37	46
7	3/8 IN POWER DRILLS	98374	144	80	100	94	118	106	132	117	147
8		92845	22	12	15	14	18	16	20	18	22
9		4554	81	45	56	53	66	59	74	66	83
10		9835	160	89	111	105	131	118	147	131	163
11		245	414	230	288	271	339	304	380	337	422
12	1/2 IN POWER DRILLS	651	95	53	66	63	78	70	88	78	97
13		859451	22	12	15	14	18	16	20	18	22
14	HAMMER DRILS	87233	14	8	10	9	12	11	13	12	15
15		4432	18	10	13	12	15	13	17	15	18

List on a spreadsheet the key items you are going to chase. Hopefully, you can use something similar from one of your existing inventory programs. It is too much of a project to do this for each item. Pick just the main ones.

Take the list and make a column for LY sales by week. In the next column, insert a formula for how much you anticipate the sales to increase each week, or just hand jam your number. You may wish to round up for an easier view. Our example shows four weeks. You should be able to do this for up to 16 weeks out.

Now you have a list of key SKUs and your anticipated sales, matched to a floor map. Every store has their system of how you order merchandise. Work with your boss and the system to order these items. Do not program the merchandise to come in at once. Program the shipments to arrive once or twice per week.

This does take some follow-up action to review the actual sales. You will need to make adjustments based on sales. If an item is selling out you can order more or get a similar product. Be careful of stacking up excess.

Many stores have a program set up for automatic replenishment. Make it a part of your Battle Rhythm to review each four foot section of your store twice or more each year to ensure you have the correct flow set up.

Know what items in your store you can never run out of. Every store has a set of basic items you must always have, such as wooden spoons in a kitchen gadget section. Nobody was ever hurt by ordering an extra box of wooden spoons.

4. SELL FROM A FULL FLOOR

When a customer comes into your store, you need to present them with full shelves. You need to look like you are in business.

Sears made a strategic mistake years ago. Their CEO, Eddie Lampert, wanted to keep inventory low in an effort to free up money to invest elsewhere. Their same store sales were already on a downward trend. The near barren shelves hastened their demise. Customers walked through the stores had the feeling of a store going out of business. The look became the reality.

Get your shelves looking like you are in business.

Order into items that are non-perishable basic items, like wooden spoons and plain cutting boards for a kitchen gadget section. Plan to use these items to fill shelves as you sell down on seasonal items. These are also good items to "hold" shelve space as you are waiting for other goods to arrive.

Always have end caps and key selling areas full with a sign. Keep a stock of those basic items to fill up an end cap that sold through.

Your order planning will be paramount to keeping that full look.

5. STOCKROOM MANAGEMENT

You don't sell from the stockroom. Having a well-stocked back room has never made a big impact on sales. But a mismanaged backroom cuts deep into the profits.

Use the backroom space to assist you in managing the flow of merchandise from the receiving area to the selling floor. Map out your stockroom as you did your selling floor. When you are programing in the merchandise orders, take into account how the stockroom will accommodate the flow.

Keeping stockrooms neat is one tough task. Sections will somehow become dumping grounds for whatever reason.

Set standards and enforce them.

Provide a stockroom setup that has adequate shelving and aisle space to maneuver. Have the right ladders, forklifts, pallet jacks and cranks to safely move the merchandise.

Assign a single person to be responsible. The receiving manager is often the best choice.

You need to walk the stockrooms daily. District Managers must walk them on every store visit. Praise someone if the place looks good. Mentor someone if it is a mess.

You must avoid putting clearance items in the stockroom. Same goes for the leftover seasonal merchandise. These are goods you want to be gone. Work with your buyers to do almost anything to get rid of them. Marking them down to a dollar is often better. Keeping them in the backroom wastes manpower moving them and increases the chance of damages.

Poorly managed stockrooms are often a major factor in shrink.

6. CONCLUSION

The management of your inventory becomes the cornerstone of sales and profit. District Managers and Store Managers must focus a large part of their weekly efforts on inventory management. Doing so will thrust your stores in the lead.

Mission Essential Task 7
Selling Floor

1. INTRODUCTION

To establish a selling floor that presents your merchandise for sale to the customer. Your selling floor is the physical location where the customer will select and purchase the merchandise. This MET centers on the physical setup of the selling floor which has an impact on how the customer will perceive your level of service. The selling floor offers you a chance to increase revenue through both product awareness and impulse purchases.

This is where the customer walks through and picks out the merchandise you are selling.

> **Your selling floor is a stage in an elaborate production**

Most of your efforts as an Operational Level manager are focused on the creation of your stage.

The selling floor brings together the flow of merchandise, customer service, stock selection, loss prevention, inventory control, employee productivity, and your customer base. The selling floor will be the object of your Action Plans. It bears the fruit of your successful problem solving techniques. It is a reflection of your team and store.

One day a VP was talking with a group of store managers. He wanted to re-merchandise an area of the stores. He commented that when we do this, the sales spike for about 90 days then drop off again. However, the only time the section is cleaned and resigned is when re-merchandizing effort is made. This might help explain the sales spike.

Then 90 days later it's back to the old condition.

A clean, well stocked and well signed selling floor makes a difference. Operational Level managers must provide the resources to get this accomplished.

2. MAP THE FLOOR

As discussed in Inventory Management, The first step in managing your selling floor is to make a detailed map. Make a base map that has every four foot section. Keep an original and make some copies to write on.

> **If an Infantry Soldier could only carry one piece of paper with her, it would be a local map.**

Map the items

Write what each four foot section has by category. You probably don't have time to write the SKU for every item. If you do, call us; you're missing out on setting priorities of work.

Map the sales

This is the same map we described on page 80. Use the P&L to write the sales for each section. A good unit of measure is to use the average weekly sales over the past quarter. Calculate the sales per square foot in each department. This will give you a good visual on where you are making money. You should start to see areas of opportunity.

Map the traffic

Walk your floor on a busy day. Mark your map for the areas that have the highest foot traffic. The most likely areas are by the entrance, escalators, or intersections.

Use the maps to guide your decisions. This will be used to drive your action plans for areas to exploit and improve. It will drive your ordering and the staffing.

You are to be a subject matter expert on the characteristics of your selling floor. You must know it better than anyone. District Managers need to review the maps every time you visit a store.

Use the maps as a guide for where to place items. There may be some low selling/ low profit items that you need to carry. Place these in low traffic / low selling areas.

Want to increase sales on an item? Place it in the productive areas. This might be an item you want to draw people in with, such as pink flamingos.

Place high profit items in the key areas. Low profit items to the back. Put your skills to work in setting adjacencies that flow.

3. MAKE IMPRESSIONS

Your selling floor is the impression of your entire company. Make it an awesome experience. But get real. If your entire floor is off the chart awesome every day all year round you are fooling yourself. Just focus on keeping some of your key spots 100% all the time and you will be posting some damn good numbers.

What makes a good impression?

- Build end caps with a single well priced item.
- Build end caps with an ensemble.
- A center floor display with the local football team merchandise.
- Setup a demonstration with the latest gadget.

Unresourced impressions that go bad fast:

> A gift wrap station that has one employee and a long line.
> A demonstration table with no demonstrator.
> A built out end cap with no pricing.
> An ensemble end cap missing some of the pieces.

4. DRIVE YOUR STRATEGIC EFFORTS

You are the bridge between the Strategic Level and the Tactical Level.

Find out what the Strategic Level Goals and Objectives are for your company. Most likely, there is some focus they wish to place on the selling floor. They are going after a market.

Those goals are often communicated through to the District Managers. Read them. Digest them. Own them. Find out some of the WHY behind the communications.

If the communication is not there - go find it. It's out there.

Then take that Strategic Level intent and put it into action on your selling floor.

Are they looking to increase sales on high margin merchandise? Put those high margin items on your end caps and front windows.

Are they looking to outsell a competitor in a category? Put that item out front with balloons. Reinforce it with staff training and communication to let them know its importance.

District Mangers must have semi-annual discussions with leadership on what focus to put out on the selling floor. Asking the question - What impression does this company want to portray to our customers?

5. FLOOR CHECKLISTS

A clean well stocked, and well signed selling floor makes a difference.

> **Task:** Use a checklist to walk the selling floor and look for key points.
>
> **Purpose:** To ensure your selling floor is suited to provide the customer with a pleasant shopping experience.

The Task / Purpose is NOT to have a checklist filled out at the end of the night.

We have a set of simple checklists in this chapter. The checklists listed here are just a starting point. You will need to expand them to meet the needs of your specific store. Griffin Gorge Associates offers a service to work with your stores to develop effective checklists.

MET 7: Selling Floor

It is tough to make a checklist that works across all stores. Grocery stores have a whole host of issues to look at in regards to fresh meats and produce. Other stores like pharmacies have expiration dates and stock rotation concerns to add in their floor walks.

The checklists should have details for key points to look at when reviewing your sales floor. It walks through all of the things to look at for having your sales floor conducive to the customer. It is detailed, but you break it down into a few manageable sections.

Make these checklists a part of your Battle Rhythm. Integrate the checklists into the floor supervisor's daily tasks.

Do not just give someone the checklist and tell them to walk the selling floor and check each area. Doing this will just waste time and a good piece of paper - a loss prevention issue now.

Have the person read it - set it down and go walk the floor. Really take some time to see how you look to the customer. The checklist is a guide for what to look at. Teach your supervisors what right looks like.

The next few pages has a series of checklists for your selling floor. Expand on these for your store to keep the standards high on your stage. These will ensure you are focused on the important things.

A checklist only works if you:

1. Make it part of the Battle Rhythm
2. Provide the resources to work it

It is always good to rotate the checklists around to different people. A second set of eyes will always find improvements.

Use the checklist for targeted areas of your store. Do not have a person use the checklist to walk the entire store in a morning. This is a bad idea that will generate bad results. Cover the entire store - one section at a time.

Once you have enforced the Battle Rhythm of walking the checklist, you must provide the resources needed to make any corrections. The checklist is a form of communication that something is out of line. As a leader, you need to direct the resources to fix it. Use some of the problem solving skills in Mission Essential Task 10 to tackle any systemic problems.

Griffin Gorge Associates
To Sell Merchandise At A Profit

A District Manager Checklist

Each DM must have a checklist of items to look at each time you visit a store. Develop a separate checklist for each store. Share the checklist with the Store Manager.

You are a very busy person and your time is valuable when you are out visiting your stores. A checklist will allow the Store Manager to have some things ready for you. It helps to enforce your standards on the store. It targets your discussions and coaching. It brings some continuity and uniformity in the selling floors across several stores.

Sample Checklists (a starter pack)

SELLING FLOOR

All items priced	
Sales correctly marked	
Organized by size	
Shelves and racks full	
Items are neatly on the shelf/rack/hood	
Packaging neat	
Shelves are clean	
Displays are neat and signed	
If it is displayed - is it stocked next to it	
If it is stocked - is it displayed next to it	
Accessories next to the main end item	
If it's part of a set - do you have all the parts	
Registers clearly identified	
Neat register area	
Carts in good shape	
Shopping baskets	
Aisle and overhead signs	
Front window displays - change twice per month	
No blocked areas or isles.	
Overhead signs	

Larger stores will need to have different checklist for each section.

MET 7: Selling Floor

You facilities are a part of the stage that is your selling floor. Walk these and make sure they meet your standards. If the landlord is responsible to fix it - you be responsible to lean on him to do his job. Take charge as a leader and make sure your store is ready for your customers.

FACILITIES

Vacuumed, mopped and dusted	
Lighting	
Restrooms	
Do walls need to be painted?	
Carpet and floor look appealing	
Store front	
Parking lot	
Walkways leading to the store	
Entrance sign	
Do you smell	
Temperature control	
Background music	
Power outage plan	

MISSION ESSENTIAL TASK 8
COMPETITION

1. INTRODUCTION

To gain an understanding of the establishments that are in competition for your customers. In a marketplace where there are multiple locations and avenues for the sale of merchandise, businesses will compete for customers. Successful businesses will gain customers by establishing a level of service above their competition through physical location, product selection, customer service and perception of value. This MET centers on gaining an edge on your competition by knowing who they are, where they are and their capabilities. You must understand them in a way to exploit their weaknesses and to defend against their strengths.

Know them then kill them.

Your competition is out there sucking business away from you. They are preventing you from selling more. They are taking away your opportunity to expand.

Guide your business to outflank them. Spear them in the side and kick them in the soft spot.

You will only beat your competition if you do two things:
-Study them
-Guide your business to be ahead of them

2. THE THREAT

The threat of your competitions comes from a few different sources.

    a. **Product selection**: The customer's desire to purchase an item often starts with their need to select a product. They may desire a new product through advertising; such as seeing the new item on TV. They may be seeking a replacement or upgrade to a current possession. In any case, they seek to go forth and make a purchase. You need to view at your competitors and determine if they are offering a better selection.

    b. **Physical location**: The type and cost of the merchandise may determine how far the customer is willing to travel to make the purchase. This includes the convenience of ordering online. There is the convenience of taking 30 minutes to go to your store now instead of waiting a few days. Also take into account commuting patterns that influence their decision.

    c. **Customer service:** The customer needs some basic level of customer service to get the merchandise. This may simply come from placing an order online and having a robot pick-pack-ship. Determine what value of customer service you offer, what your competition offers and what the customer desires.

d. **Perception of Value:** Price points are often the first perception the customer has regarding value. The real question is "Does the customer feel they got a product worth the time, effort and money?"

3. STUDY THE COMPETITION

Your Strategic Office will be watching the competition. They will do their job in looking at the five year plan to push your company into the lead. Trust them.

You can do a lot on the Operational Level. Make a binder or folder on the competition in your area.

Think here - where are your customers and where are the other places they can purchase the merchandise you are selling?

Physical Stores

   List: Gather the names and location of the stores that sell your merchandise. If you sell frames, where are all the frame stores your customers could shop? This list of stores might have to be sorted by product category.

   Map: Put up a map specifically for your competition. Impose this over commuting routes and high trafficked road networks. A competitor's distance is not as important as the frequency your customers are driving past them. This will aid you in targeting.

   Visit: Go out and visit the competition. Make notes on how they stack up against your store. Use the checklists you have to walk your selling floor. Write down comments. You can have some of your staff go do the visits.

   Research: Conduct some research on the completion. Find out how committed they are to your market. Note if they are new and expanding. Maybe they are entrenched. Note how financially stable the company. Dig into finding what investors are writing about their future.

   Rate: Rate each of the stores on how much of a threat you perceive them to be.

   Strengths & Weaknesses: List some of the strengths and weakness you found in your competition.

   Action: Now, write out where you can exploit your competition's weakness and where you need to shore up against their strengths. Turn this into some of your Objectives. Make a solid plan to go after your competition. A plan to adjust your business in a way to pull customers from them. Priorities should be based on going after the competitors you rated as the biggest threat.

Online Shopping

This is a tough one.

<u>List:</u> Make a list of the key items in your store that customers can easily, and most likely, will purchase online. If you sell lollipops, most likely that is not an online purchase. If you sell tractors, that is most likely not an online purchase. Tractor accessories would be a strong candidate for an online purchase - let's use this as our example.

<u>Shop:</u> Scan the online retailers for sites that sell tractor accessories.

<u>Compare:</u> Note the brand you have and who else is selling it.

<u>Attack:</u> Write down the strengths you have over the online retailer. If they beat you on price for the same item, how can you grab that sale - and do it in the best interest of the customer? Our section in ethics stresses you need to act in a way that is best for the customer, not you. Dig deep and be imaginative. Maybe, you cost a few bucks more but have free installation.

<u>Communicate:</u> If the online deal is just too good for you to compete with, communicate that with your Strategic Office. Contact your buyer and discuss it. Maybe they can work some promotional deal during the busy season (2 for 1, discounts, etc) or even negotiate a price reduction with the vendor.

4. INDUSTRY TRENDS

Sometimes, the competition is a new paradigm. A great example is the advent of online shopping. That became a game changing event for almost all brick and mortar stores.

Your industry will be trending. Things always change. Keep abreast of what your industry news is saying.

If you sell sporting goods, what are the trends for that product line? If you operate a store in a mall, what are the trends for mall retailers in your area and nationwide?

You are selling merchandise. Is your merchandise still needed by the customer? This is a question more directed to the Strategic Office to wrestle with. But it affects you and you need to be aware of your surroundings.

You do not need to do in depth research here. Your Strategic Office should be. However, you do need to have situational awareness of the bigger picture.

5. CONCLUSION

Never underestimate your competition. It is very dynamic. A competitor that does not pose a threat today could eat your lunch tomorrow. A new upstart could sweep past you. The dimwit you past last year could polish itself.

> **"They couldn't hit an elephant at this distance."**
> Major General John Sedgwick moments before being killed by a sniper
> May 9th, 1864.

MISSION ESSENTIAL TASK 9
LOSS PREVENTION

1. INTRODUCTION

To protect company resources (manpower and funds) from being expended on unnecessary events. Your store generates revenue through the sale of merchandise. The revenue is funneled to pay for expenses and to invest in growth. The balance is your profit. Any expenditure of resources that is not a valued expense or investment is a corresponding loss to profit. Operational Level leaders are responsible for most of the venues where resources are lost. This MET centers on places where leaders must identify where there are losses, or potential losses, and put measures in place to prevent them.

Loss prevention is a lot more than preventing some crackhead from running away with a shirt.

> **Loss Prevention**
> **Preventing any money or resource from leaving your store unless it provides a value in return**

You take money out of your store to pay your staff. You are losing money but with the understanding you are getting something more in return.

You spend money to pay rent and utility bills. These are all good things to spend money on. For if you don't pay rent and utility bills, the store is not long for this world.

Task: Identify and then reduce or eliminate the spending on something that does not provide a value in return.

Purpose: To increase profits and allow for resources to be utilized in a way that does provide a value in return.

The first step is to identify where you are losing money. There are many aspects to search. In the sections below, we cover some of the most common loss prevention issues.

Every store is different!

To find the most obvious, review your P&L to find out where your store is out of line with comparable stores.

MET 9: Loss Prevention

Next, walk and observe the actions in your store. Employee productivity, employee attentiveness to their surroundings, and employee attentiveness to doing the processes correctly.

Once you identify the areas you are losing money, do what a leader does. Commit the resources towards fixing the problem. This may be doing some simple steps or coaching. In some cases, you will go through the full Problem Solving Process detailed in Mission Essential Task 10.

In regards to Loss Prevention, a leader will:

1. Identify the weakness.
2. Find the best solution.
3. Commit the resources to fix it.
4. Enforce the standards.
5. Follow-up for improvements.
6. Share the lesson learned.

You will never eliminate your loss prevention issues. You must strive hard to mitigate them or they will put you out of business.

2. EMPLOYEE ACCIDENTS

Employee accidents are often the biggest loss you can prevent. In fact, employee accidents are the absolute worse for loss for two reasons. First, someone got hurt. It is just not good to see people get hurt. Second, the cost in medical care, lost productivity, and worker compensation claims add up fast after just minor accidents.

A store, or any business, with high accident rates will start to suffer secondary effects such as lower moral, and lower productivity. This can often foster an environment of employee sabotage by design or default. When employees see that their company truly does not care about them when they keep getting injured, they will return the favor.

3. UTILITY BILLS

Quarterly (on your Battle Rhythm) review your utility bills. Check for unusual spikes or changes. Walk your store to see where you can make cuts.

But do not make cuts so deep they hurt. One store had the bright idea to keep almost all the lights off until the opening bell. And off again at the closing bell. A lot of productivity was lost with employees trying just to see. It was almost like a comedy show. People running around with flashlights stocking shelves and doing price changes. The short sighted manager was proud of having the lowest electric bill in the company. He failed to walk the floor and listen to the staff complain. And complain with a valid reason.

> ### Story of Angelo
>
> Angelo was the manager of a store doing about $52 million in annual sales during the 1980s. The staff consisting of full and part timers was about 200 strong. He reviewed the annual P&L after his first year in office. In a well-planned maneuver, he assembled his key staff. The estimated loss from theft was about $50,000. The actual loss in employee accidents was over $250,000.
>
> He said the cold math shows the store would come out ahead if we allowed twice the theft and reduced the accidents by just a third. As a side bonus he noted we just might end up not getting ourselves hurt.
>
> Angelo directed the Loss Prevention team to turn their entire focus on improving safety.
>
> Attitudes changed fast. Managers started to provide resources for workplace safety. Better forklifts, better ladders, non-killing box cutters (this is way in the days before standards). Managers enforcing workplace safety by stopping employees from climbing shelves and balancing on chairs. Signing wet floors. Most importantly, managers gave more time to complete some tasks such as unloading freight and breaking down boxes.
>
> Unsafe acts resulted in disciplinary actions. An employee was found swinging on a raised forklift fork while his buddies watched and laughed. A clear message was sent when he got terminated (sounds harsh but it was not his first infraction).
>
> One year later, the cost for employee accidents was cut in half and remained on a downward trend. Success breeds success. Theft losses remained the same.
>
> Be like Angelo. He studied the problem, developed a sound solution, implemented the plan, enforced the plan, and increased profits while improving employee health.

4. LEAN SIX SIGMA PRINCIPLES

Employee productivity.

You can really step up your game (profits) by studying your employee productivity.

Key leaders need to take a short course on the LSS process. Read a book, watch a YouTube video, or take an online course. An effective tactic could be using the LSS classes as incentive within your team to develop leaders.

MET 9: Loss Prevention

Task: Become familiar with LSS process and terms.

Purpose: To apply some of those principles to your store operations on order to increase productivity.

Find areas in your store that will benefit from a productivity review:

- Receiving
- Stocking
- Inventory management
- Front End Registers
- Store Opening/Closing procedures
- Cash out procedures

Take a day or two dedicated to taking your employee routines. Look for ways they can improve without sacrificing your standards.

Look for what resources you can provide that will allow them to perform their jobs faster, better, safer. A really god idea is to just ask them.

A solid Objective for any store would be to pick a section or process in your store to improve using the LSS principles.

5. RETURNS

Previously in Mission Essential Task 3 Customer Service, we discussed how returns are a way to increase your business in the long term. That is a true statement. However, you will increase your level of customer service and profit if you can reduce selling merchandise that is destined to become a return.

Reduce Selling Items That End Up Being Returned

You will greatly increase your profits if you are able to reduce the level of returns.

This is a good place to go through the full Problem Solving Process covered in Mission Essential Task 10.

Go gather the Facts and make some solid Assumptions. Move into developing Courses Of Action to fix the problems.

This starts with going to your return desk and doing some simple analysis on why customers are returning items. Be methodical about this. Take a look at your P&L. What section has the highest return rate? Dig into the details. You will most likely find several underlying factors. Then, talk to the salesmen out on the floor and discuss the problems.

Next, take a look at the section of your store with the lowest return rate. Try to find out why. There may be some very good things happening there that can be duplicated.

District Managers need to step in and compare the return rates in your stores using some of the same comparisons. Do you have a store way out of line (good or bad)? Do you have a trend across your stores?

By analyzing your returns and fixing the problem, you have a direct impact on preventing loss.

Properly Process Returns

Once you do have returns coming in the door, they need to be quickly and efficiently processed. Walk into a store and look at piles of returns around the customer service area. This indicates poor leadership.

Take your skills learned in the LSS and work on improving the flow of your returned merchandise.

First, make sure the cashier is recording why the merchandise is returned.

Second, have a qualified employee validate the reason - but not in front of the customer.

Third, get it moving along back to the selling floor or into the return bins in the back room.

The return bin in the back room must be cleaned out regularly. Set it into your store Battle Rhythm. Once per week or two weeks at the most.

The preferred option is Return To Vendor (RTV) and getting some type of credit. Make sure you take advantage of this as much as possible. Most likely the buyers have negotiated this into the contract. If you do not take advantage of it, your company paid for a service you did not use.

A point here is to not allow returns to pile up near the return desk nor in the back room. This invites multiple problems. First, time erodes your ability to get it back to the floor with further damage. You could lose vendor credit if they have stipulated a time frame.

Importantly, your employees will see you are serious about taking care of your inventory. When employees see you enforcing standards, it spreads to other areas. When employees see you not enforcing the standards, they will follow your lead.

6. EMPLOYEE THEFT

Employee theft is among one of the worse problems to deal with when running a store. As a natural human occurrence, when people are working with each other on a daily basis, friendships are built. Even if there are no interactions outside of the workplace, you get to know each other's families, interests and lives.

Then you find they are stealing. It cuts to a personal level; more is lost than what they stole.

Most likely by the time you catch them, they have done some real damage. Like a cockroach sucking termite, they have eaten through some beams before you find the sawdust.

Prevent It

The first step in dealing with employee theft is to put measures in place to prevent it. The District Managers and Store Managers must set high standards for their store operations.

The most important standard is cleanliness. A well maintained store will have lower theft. Read the article "Broken Windows" by James Q. Wilson and George Kelling, The Atlantic Monthly (March 1982).

Enforce the standards of taking good care of your inventory. Shelves are neat and cleaned. The backroom is neat. Boxes are placed in designated locations and waste is disposed of properly. This will also aid in identifying problems early.

Monitor your front end and receiving. Make sure the employees are following all of the store policies.

Have discussions with your floor managers on ways to prevent employee theft.

Discuss having cameras placed in locations such as the receiving dock and stock rooms. Make sure the employees know they are there. Many times this is all you need to prevent theft.

Remember, you are seeking to prevent theft. You are not out to set people up and catch them in the act.

Bag checks when employees are leaving is a great deterrent. Set the standards by having an employee check your bag.

If your company has a loss prevention / security team, work with that leadership at the Strategic Level to find out what other stores are doing. Ask for the stories behind some of the employee theft cases from across the company. This makes for a good read and will give you some ideas on prevention.

Monitor For It

You need to monitor your P&L and your inventory to identify problems early. This is a very hard thing to do. It takes time form a busy day to scan for this. You will find yourself searching for nothing most of the time. But at least do it on occasion.

When an employee is stealing, they often are only stealing in the area they work in. It calls too much attention for them to steal from areas they do not belong in. A dock worker stealing is not up in your front end shorting a register.

Deal With It Properly

Once you find or suspect an employee stealing - notify your supervisor and get advice. Do not tackle this on your own. Call or email your boss about the problem immediately. Unless someone's life is in danger, corrective actions can wait a couple of days.

Your boss will raise it through their supervisors. The company Loss Prevention team will most likely have specific protocols to follow. Your company lawyers should be reviewing those protocols.

Do not discuss the theft with anyone except your boss. Do not call your friends, other peers nor the thief's supervisor.

After calling your boss, write down everything that lead you to discovering the theft. Get the details. Keep this filed in a locked drawer. If written on a computer, make sure it is not a file others can access. Give it to your Loss Prevention team when they arrive.

If someone was with you when you made the discovery, have them write the details in their own words and instruct them not to discuss it.

7. EMPLOYEE ATTENTIVENESS

Your employees need to be attentive in two areas.

Be Aware Of Your Surroundings

Being aware of your surroundings improves the store's loss prevention a several ways. The employees will notice thefts as they happen, or at least identify the problem quickly afterwards.

Employees will also notice safety issues when they are aware of their surroundings.

How do you get them to do this?

You bring this up during regular store meetings or morning huddles. Just mentioning it in a few short sentences goes a long way.

When walking the store and engaging the staff in conversation, mention the importance of being aware of the surroundings. Require your subordinate managers do the same.

Provide positive reinforcement when an employee notices something and brings attention to get it fixed.

MET 9: Loss Prevention

Be Attentive To Doing Processes Correctly

Your employees conduct many processes daily. The receive merchandise off the trucks, they price the goods, they ring on the registers, they count the money, etc.

Give them the time to do the processes correctly. Enforce that they do them correctly. People will follow your example. If you cut corners, you have established the norm. If you witness someone cutting corners and do not take any action, you have established the norm.

If you see something wrong and do not correct it, you let everyone know you do not care about it.

Many of the processes your store has in place are there to properly account for the merchandise and the money. There are some good reasons they are in place. Take the time to learn them yourself.

If you see a process that is not effective, is outdated, or needs to be improved - you need to raise it to your boss. Be clear in your communication. Write it out in a formal letter. Specify the current process, demonstrate why it is of no value and then offer a solution. If you just complain and say these steps are useless; then you are too.

If you do send a formal letter to your boss seeking an improvement, while you are waiting for an answer, you continue to do the process the old way.

8. THIEVES

People will come into your store and steal every time you open your doors.

Crackheads, housewives, businessmen, students, working stiffs, well dressed, raggity ass, smelly, well spoken, couples, singles, groups, friendly, grumpy, with or without teeth, long hair, short hair, bald, tall, short, in a hurry and slow moving.

If you work in retail long enough, you will find there is absolutely no group or click that lacks a shoplifter.

Having a presence on the selling floor and demonstrating an awareness is the single biggest deterrent. Other deterrents include a clean and well-lit selling floor.

Once the deterrents fail, follow your stores policy regarding shoplifters.

Do not branch off on your own.

Have discussions with your store's Loss Prevention team and discuss the correct way to deal with the thief.

But here are some absolute do's and don'ts when you encounter a thief:

- Assume you are wrong in your assumption. It is bad for business to ever accuse an innocent customer of theft. On the big picture, if they are stealing less than a truck load (LTL), a wrong accusation is not worth the goods they are taking.

- No one gets in trouble for being nice. If the thief is still in the store, offer them a soda. Offer the people in the area a soda to show you are not playing favorites. Or a coupon. Or popcorn. Or something that would make an innocent customer happy.

- Don't follow them around right on their heels.

Just as every grouping of people has a shoplifter, most people in every group are not shoplifters.

Your store Loss Prevention team most likely has policies regarding customer theft. Follow it.

9. LISTEN TO THE STAFF

The inherent desire for most employees to see the business succeed. Engage them on conversions about your store. They will often have ideas about preventing a loss you never knew you were having.

Loss prevention is all about getting to keep your profits

Mission Essential Task 10
Problem Solving

1. INTRODUCTION

To solve problems such that your decisions provide the best outcome for your company in terms of revenue and profit. Operational Level leaders are required to conduct problem solving techniques several times a day. These problems require you to render a decision. At times, these problems will generate a decision that has far reaching effects for the growth and profitability of the business. This MET centers on teaching Operational Level leaders the foundations of becoming a master at established problem solving techniques. Once practiced, these techniques will ensure you are making decisions that result in the best available outcome.

Planning and Problem Solving are the two greatest traits of a strong leader.

The problem solving process shown here is adapted from the Military Decision Making Process (MDMP). This process was designed, tested and refined over many years by high level academia and Soldiers out in the trenches. This process works.

The processes shown in this chapter is in the public domain and is not copyrighted.

The process outlined here will cost you a few hours this week and save you days of pain in 6 months. Put in a few extra hours this week and save days of work later; end up with money and profits. Skip this now; enjoy a few hours of laziness today then in a few months enjoy some pain and working late.

By taking the time to go through these steps, you will have a better run organization and will be more efficient with your resources. Learn and master problem solving. Soon you will find yourself ahead of your competitors.

This chapter shows the full length version of problem solving. Time constraints might prevent you from completing all the steps. But take time to learn each of these steps in detail. Become a master. Take time to learn it and practice it on small problems. Once you master this process, when you make small decisions, you will intuitively run though the steps. Always use the long way when solving a complicated problem, or a problem that will have a significant impact.

Properly solving a problem and implementing the best course of action does not mean you have eliminated any bad consequences. When you are done with the problem solving and have a decision, you still will deal with negative consequences. Understand that. Mitigate them.

2. PROCESS OVERVIEW

Let's show a short recap of how the process works, then we will dive into the details.

Start by writing:

> **What is the problem?**
> **What is your Desired End State?**

Then prepare to seek guidance from your leadership

> **Guidance Briefing**

Take their guidance, fully analyze the problem and develop a Course of Action (COA)

> **Problem Analysis & COA Development**

Go to your leadership with the proposed COA and explain how you arrived at this. Seek their approval for your COA.

> **Decision Briefing**

Once the COA is approved, write out a plan to get it done.

> **Operations Plan**

Ensure your staff understands what the plan is and follow-up on the action.

> **Communicate & follow-up**

The speed at which this progresses will depend on the scope of the problem. We have seen sound decisions for small problems produced in an hour. Complicated and intense problems can take 14 days of round the clock grinding for a team of 120 Soldiers working in concert.

The Problem Solving Steps

3. IDENTIFY THE PROBLEM

The real first step is knowing you have a problem that needs solving. But let's just skip to the step where you know there is a problem.

You will most likely be looking at a symptom and not the real problem. Then ask why three times deep. You want to solve the right problem.

We will follow the example of company having a problem in excess inventory at the end of a season. Do not get wrapped around the details here. The lesson is about the process.

In this scenario - you are part of a team that is making a decision for the VP to approve. This would be problem solving as a collaborative effort.

This starts out as a true story...

The VP was once sitting in an office in Manhattan with about a dozen store managers. He was asking how to deal with the plethora of clearance inventory in the stores. Everyone piped up and started making all kinds of crazy talk. Suggesting consolidating it all to a couple of stores and marking it down. A few said mark it down "aggressively" and have a week long push to clear it out. Basically a bunch of smart people throwing poop in the air. Sitting around the table and the first one to get the VP to say "That's a good idea" wins the prize.

Good smart professional people - just not properly trained in solving a problem.

Someone said take the inventory outside; with a little kerosene and a match we can solve this problem. Our collective salary sitting here talking about it and the cost of a hundred employees marking it down is more expensive. Whatever answer you are trending towards still has us back here next year.

The real problem he said, is how they ended up with so much fudging excess inventory (only he didn't say fudge). Buyers gone crazy is the issue. They are getting a good deal buying in bulk and are not communicating with the stores on how to sell it before the end of the season. The stores have large orders coming in with no coordination on how to move it off the shelves.

Ask the why three times. Now you are starting to identify the real problem. Don't solve a symptom of the problem - or you will revisit it in six months.

Griffin Gorge Associates
To Sell Merchandise At A Profit

We have too much inventory.

    why - the buyers bought too much in bulk orders
        why- the vendors only give discounts after $X million in purchases
            why didn't the stores sell all of it?

    There was no communication or plan for the increased volume of merchandise.

We will follow this example of excess seasonal inventory.

Now pretend the 12 store managers get together to properly and professionally solve this problem. How do we do this?

Identify the problem and work through to **what you want to accomplish.** What is your desired End State?

Problem Statement
Seasonal inventory is being shipped to the stores in quantities exceeding the stores ability to sell through before the end of the season.

Task-Purpose (write out what you want to do)
Reduce the amount of excess inventory at the end of the season // in order to minimize the amount of money lost through markdowns.

Desired End State (Objective) (write out what you desire to accomplish)
The company sells seasonal merchandise at a profit and the end of season inventory shall not exceed 5% of total seasonal inventory purchased.

Stakeholders
Strategic-Operational-Tactical
You are on the Operational Level. Stuck in the middle. Get a stakeholder on the bookends - Strategic and Tactical

Even if you do not bring them in on the problem solving, list all who will be impacted or have an effect on this.

- Buyers
- Vendors
- Store Managers
- Salesman

Side Note: If this group stayed on the wrong track to solve the issue of the current problem of excess inventory, the time and resources expended would have been wasted. That is a Loss Prevention issue.

--Print the following page and hang it up--

PROBLEM SOLVING

1. Identify The Problem
Ask the question "why" three times deep. Find a root cause. Write out what you really want to accomplish.
    Problem Statement
    Task
    Purpose
    <u>Desired End State (Objective)</u>
    Stakeholders

2. Leadership Guidance
Present the problem to your leadership. The purpose is to get their approval to commit resources to the solution and get their initial guidance. (The Guidance Brief)

3. Analyze The Problem
The most important step.
    a. Facts
    b. Assumptions
    c. Specified Tasks
    d. Implied Tasks
    e. Essential Tasks
    f. Constraints
    g. Assets Available
    h. Resource Shortfalls
    i. Risks
    j. Timeline

4. Develop Courses of Action (COA)
Look at your analysis and outline three courses of action. Each must be:
a. Feasible   b. Acceptable   c. Suitable   d. Distinguishable

5. Define the Rating Criteria
List 3-6 criteria that will be used to make the decision.
Write the following for each criteria:
    a. Name
    b. Definition
    c. Unit of Measure
    d. Benchmark
    e. Formula
    f. Weight

6. Compare COAs
Rate the criteria and see which one objectively best meets your goal.
Build a Decision Matrix (DECMAT).

7. The Decision Brief
Write a Decision Brief for the leadership. They need to clearly understand the scope of the problem and to make a decision for a COA.

8. Write The Operations Plan
Write out a coherent structured plan to get this all done. Synchronize the stakeholder actions. Literally speaking - get everyone on the same page.

9. Implement The Plan
    a. Disseminate it
    b. Get a Backbrief
    c. Validate actions being taken
    d. Follow-up
    e. Refine

As you move through the process, adjust, refine and change the information to add clarity and remove ambiguity. Make this a useful product.

4. LEADERSHIP GUIDANCE

Use the Guidance Briefing format and go discuss it with the VP.

    Task: Provide the leadership with an outline of the problem you are seeking to solve.

    Purpose: To gain their concurrence to proceed towards a solution. Also, to gain their input for guidance and expectations.

This is designed to give your leadership the foundation of the problem, your outline to solve it and importantly - to get their initial guidance. **At this point you are not working on solutions. You are identifying the scope of the problem and articulating where you want to end up.**

If you are working on a large problem, it is important to get your leadership's input at the start of the process. The solution will often incur the commitment of significant resources and change current business practices.

If this is a smaller problem, one that you are solving without your leadership, still draft a Guidance Briefing. It will help you focus your efforts.

GUIDANCE BRIEF

This is used to inform your leadership on a problem you are seeking to solve. Use this to gain their guidance before proceeding into developing a detailed Course of Action (COA) to solve the problem.

1. Situation.
Briefly describe the current conditions and circumstances that the plan addresses.

    a. <u>Area</u>
Identify the stores / districts / states effected by this plan.

    b. <u>Stakeholders</u>
List all of the stakeholders effected by the plan.

2. Concept of The Plan

    a. <u>Problem Statement</u>
What is the base problem being solved?

    b. <u>Leader's Intent</u>
What is the intent of the leader initiating this action?
        More to the point - what do you really want to accomplish?
This is the most important statement in the problem solving process. This will most likely be adjusted based on comments after this brief.

    c. <u>Task & Purpose</u>
WHAT are you doing and WHY are you doing it.

    d. <u>Desired End State (Objective)</u>
What is the desired outcome - be specific by using a measurable.

3. Key Event Timeline
List all of the significant dates in sequential order.

4. Conclusion
*Summarize the problem and your desired end state in one paragraph.
Ask for questions and further guidance.
Ask if there should be an In Process Review (IPR), otherwise the next meeting will be when you present the Decision Brief.*

5. ANALYZE THE PROBLEM

Once you have your leadership's guidance and approval to proceed, you need to fully analyze the problem. This is the most important step. A thorough analysis is what will give you a complete picture of what the problem involves. If this is a team effort - and the large problems will be a team effort - everyone gets busy with this part.

As they say in the old country - this is where we make the sausage.

Write down a list for the following

FACTS
(A statement that can be verified)
- Markdowns reduce profit margins
- Averaging $300,000 in markdowns per district in the 3rd quarter
- $2,000,000 in gross sales per district from the seasonal merchandise

ASSUMPTIONS
(Reasonably believe will happen or reasonably believe is true - but not confirmed. Often an expected future event)
- No actions will result in the same problem next season
- Vendors will make some accommodations

SPECIFIED TASKS
(A task specifically stated by the leadership during the Guidance Brief)
- Reduce clearance inventory at the end of the month
- We will buy 10% more red tablecloths for next season

IMPLIED TASKS
(A task that the leadership did not specify during the Guidance Brief, but you determined will need to be done)
- Conduct training on approved plan
- Better communications between Buyers and District Managers

ESSENTIAL TASKS
(A task the leadership said must be completed)
- The solution must produce a greater profit than current action

CONSTRAINTS
(Limits the leadership or nature has placed on the COA)
- Do not fundamentally change the structure of the buying process
- This is an additional task - all of us are still running our stores

ASSETS AVAILABLE
(Resources the leadership or planning group has made available for the COA)
- HR trainers will assist for implementation

RESOURCE SHORTFALLS
(Resource constraints that will limit the COA)
- No clearance centers
- No consolidation framework established

RISKS
(An event that, if it occurs, can have a negative or positive effect on the COA)
- Competition fields a new line of merchandise that is better/cheaper

TIMELINE
(Sketch out a timeline of events. This will keep everyone focused to complete each step. List only key milestones.)

2017
August 1	Complete Decision Brief
August 15	Complete the Plan
August 30	Publish the Plan
October 1	Buyers negotiate next season purchases

2018
March 1- 16	Merchandise ships to stores
March 2-20	Stores set up selling floor
April1 - June 30	Season
July 1	Begin end of season clearance
July 15	Clearance sales complete; closes season

6. DEVELOP COURSES OF ACTION (COA)

a. **Define a COA**: A COA is a broad potential solution to an identified problem. Try to come up with three. Be flexible in through the process. Your final decision might have a bit of each. Each COA must be:

(1) <u>Feasible</u>: The COA can be accomplished within the established time, space, and resource limitation.

(2) <u>Acceptable</u>: The COA must balance cost & risk with the advantaged gained.

(3) <u>Suitable</u>: The COA can be accomplished within the leadership's intent and planning guidance.

(4) <u>Distinguishable</u>: Each COA must differ significantly from the others.

b. Draft Three COAs

To arrive at your three COA's, the group needs to brainstorm the Problem Statement. Try to come up with different ways to solve the problem. Write out all the ideas as they come up.

As an idea is written down, it may prompt discussion on possible subordinate actions. Someone may suggest more store involvement and another leans in to say that should include training for the store managers. This is where you let, and encourage, people to develop ideas. Write all of this down.

As the ideas flow, you normally will see three COAs forming. If not, try to guide the discussion towards that.

Note: The Army teaches you to have three COAs not matter the situation. If there are only two real options, just make something up so you can throw it out later. This is BS. Don't work on BS. If there are only two then just work the two. If you develop four - run with it.

Then write down the COAs and the subordinate ideas that came out of the session. Then write a paragraph on how the COA should play out. You are not getting into the fine details yet. That will come later.

In our case of the excess inventory, we see our three COAs:

    1. Reduce the volume purchased by 10%.
The stores are having a problem selling all of the seasonal merchandise. By simply reducing the volume of goods shipped, you should see a reduction in excess.

    2. Same volume; increase store involvement.
The buyers purchase the same volume of merchandise; but include a plan to the stores on how to sell it. This should include some training to the store managers.

    3. Same volume; consolidate clearance at the end of the season.
Do the same thing next year. At the end of the season, the stores ship their excess to selected stores. The inventory is marked down to clear it out.

7. DEFINE THE RATING CRITERIA

Once you have the COAs in rough draft, you need to figure out how you will rate them against each other to determine the best way to proceed.

List 3-6 criteria that will be used to make the decision.

This is used to measure and evaluate how you will be comparing each COA. This really brings into focus which COA will give the best outcome. Never skip this.

MET 10: Problem Solving

Each criteria will have:
    Name   Give a 1-2 word title to label it
    Definition   One sentence to describe the criteria
    Unit of Measure   How will you measure this
    Benchmark   Where do you start the measure
    Formula   What change in the measure do you desire
    Weight   Rate the importance of the criteria from 1-5 (Higher is better)

Name: **Sales**
Definition: The sales volume of seasonal merchandise
Unit of Measure: The percentage change in sales for each store
Benchmark: Last years sales on seasonal merchandise
Formula: A increase in sales above 4.0% over last year is an advantage. An increase less than 3.99% is a disadvantage.
Weight: 5

Name: **Markdowns**
Definition: The markdowns taken on the merchandise after the normal selling period
Unit of Measure: The percent change of the original inventory that gets marked down
Benchmark: Last season's markdowns
Formula: A decrease in Markdowns is an advantage. An increase is a disadvantage.
Weight: 4

Name: **Manhours**
Definition: The number of hours worked by an employee(s) at each store on handling the season merchandise
Unit of Measure: The percentage change in hours expended for each store
Benchmark: Last season's estimated store manhours in handling seasonal merchandise
Formula: A decrease in Manhours is an advantage. An increase is a disadvantage
Weight: 2

Name: **Cost of Goods**
Definition: The profit margin for the goods purchased
Unit of Measure: The percentage of the markup
Benchmark: The previous 3 seasonal average markups
Formula: An increase in Markups is an advantage. A decrease is a disadvantage.
Weight: 4

8. COMPARE COURSES OF ACTION

The Decision Matrix
Take the criteria listed above and compare the expected results with each COA.

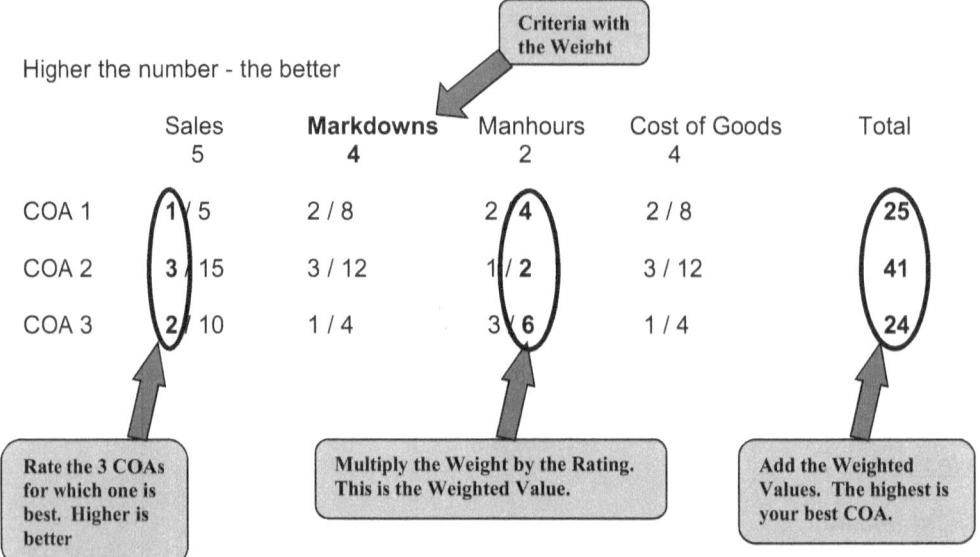

Let's look at "SALES". This is the highest weighted criteria. Since we are in the business to sell, it's a pretty important aspect. COA 1 has us purchasing less goods; so that gets the lowest rating. COA 2 anticipates that we get the same volume of goods but with a plan to sell more at the regular prices; this get the highest rating. COA 3 has the same volume as last year but anticipates about the same regular sales as last year; so this gets the middle rating.

Look at the criteria "MARKDOWNS. COA 1 and COA 3 appear like they both will have about the same in markdowns. In this example, we rated COA 1 as lower. You do have the option of rating two COAs the same if you determine there is no significant difference.

Look at the criteria "MANHOURS". Multiply the Weight by the Rating to get the Weighted Value.

You may decide to eliminate a criteria if you have a hard time finding any significant differences between the COAs. While it might be an important criteria, if no COA has a clear advantage over another, you should take it out of the formula as you are using to find a difference.

When working though the DECMAT, allow yourselves to be flexible. In the discussions, you might decide to change weights or maybe add a criteria.

You should seek to have as many stakeholders as possible review the COAs and DECMAT. More viewpoints will lead you to a better product. Just avoid the problem of diminishing returns.

Once you have selected your best COA, it's time to present this to the leadership to gain their approval to move to the next phase; which will be to produce a detailed plan

9. DECISION BRIEF

You now have determined the best COA to proceed with. You need to have your leadership make a decision based off of your hard efforts. Write a Decision Brief. Use our Decision Brief format (which we stole from the Army and then twisted it). This will show your analysis, COA development and why you came up with your proposed COA.

Some of the information on the Decision Brief is copied from the Guidance Brief.

Task: Provide the leadership with a brief review of the problem, potential COAs and your recommended COA.

Purpose: To gain their decision on a COA to correct a problem; also to gain any additional guidance.

Your VP makes $36,000 take home per paycheck; don't waste his time - it is more valuable than all of you in the room.

   a. Prepare for the briefing.

     (1) Invite the key stakeholders. All of the stakeholders should be familiar with the brief. You are presenting a COA where there may be conflicting interests and personalities. You do not want a stakeholder hearing something for the first time in the brief or asking you a tough question in front of the leadership.

> **"Surprises are for birthdays.**
> **This briefing is not a %*#@ birthday party."**
>
> **Colonel Dennis Deeley**
> **42 Infantry Division Operations Officer**

     (2) Have a good room set up. Have your presentation material all set. If you are using a Power Point or some other media, make sure it is tested out the day before.

     (3) Have a printed copy of the Decision Brief for the key people in the room.

Have the backup material with the details in order to field any questions.

(4) A rehearsal will separate the professional managers from the good ones. Be a professional.

   b. Conduct the Decision Brief.

(1) Be brief. Do not get long winded. A 50 minute brief is too long.

(2) The leadership has a printed copy of the Decision Brief. Do not read it to them. If you read line for line off a Power Point slide, do the world a favor and punch your own teeth out.

(3) Be ready to adjust your recommended COA based on additional guidance. Your leadership will evaluate the COA and how it nests with other events they are concerned with.

(4) If you get asked a tough question, do not BS the answer. If you do not have the answer just say so and tell them you will provide it as soon as possible.

(5) Depending on your leadership's style, you might not receive a concur/non-concur at the briefing.

MET 10: Problem Solving

DECISION BRIEF

The task/purpose of a Decision Brief is to present information to the leadership **to gain their decision on a course of action to correct a problem.**

This can be presented in a letter format, or this information can be transferred to a Power Point presentation. Always provide the person(s) being briefed with a written copy.

1. **Situation.**
Briefly describe the current conditions and circumstances that the plan addresses.

   a. <u>Area</u>
Identify the stores / districts / states effected by this plan.

   b. <u>Stakeholders</u>
List all of the stakeholders effected by the plan. Make note if they expected to concur/non-concur.

2. **Concept of The Plan**

   a. <u>Problem Statement</u>
What is the base problem being solved?

   b. <u>Leader's Intent</u>
What is the intent of the leader initiating this action? Simply put - what do you wan to accomplish?

   c. <u>Task & Purpose</u>
WHAT are you doing and WHY are you doing it?

   d. <u>Desired End State (Objective)</u>
What is the desired outcome - be specific by using a measurable.

3. **Recommendation**
*Briefly review the three COAs.
In a couple sentences, give the reason for your recommended COA.*

4. **Background**
In bullet points, give some of the reasons why this problem came about and what effects it is having on the company.

5. **Key Information**

   a. <u>Facts</u>
Something that actually exists.

   b. <u>Assumptions</u>
Reasonably believe will happen or reasonably believe is true - but not confirmed. Often this is a future event.

c. Specified Tasks
Tasks specified by the leadership.

d. Implied Tasks
Tasks that need to be accomplished but were not specified by the leadership.

e. Essential Tasks
Tasks the leadership said must be completed.

e. Constraints
List actions you cannot do or resources that will not be available.

f. Assets Available
What are some resources available for this plan (funding)?

f. Resource Shortfalls
Resource constraints that will limit the COA.

f. Risks
An event that, if it occurs, can have a negative or positive effect on the COA.

f. Timeline:
List the key dates in order.

f. Evaluation Criteria
This is used to measure and evaluate how you will be comparing each COA.
Each criteria will have:
Name
Definition
Unit of Measure
Benchmark
Formula
Weight
Explain how each was weighted.

6. COA
Present each of the COAs.
Explain how the Criteria was weighted for each.
Show the Decision Matrix.

7. Conclusion
Summarize your conclusion is one paragraph.
Explain any disadvantages with the COA.
You must be convincing without referring to the Decision Matrix.
Convince with a logical argument.
Ask for questions then ask for concurrence.

8. **Recommendation** *If you are using a Power Point presentation, the last slide should be the Recommendation again - exactly as the previous Recommendation slide.*

Take Action

Once you have an approved COA, you need to go do the work that will actually solve the problem.

10. WRITE THE OPERATIONS PLAN

Develop the plan details.

Here is a blueprint for a plan - stolen right out of the military joint planning guidance (Joint Publication 5-0). Adapted slightly for your company.

Task: Write a plan in using a standard format that details how your organization will commit resources to correct a problem.

Purpose: To provide a plan that is coordinated among the stakeholders and approved by the leadership. The plan provides knowledge to all stakeholders and enables them to work off of the same page. Also, it provides clear expectations to those that need to perform a task.

Once signed/approved by the VP, this will give you the authority to commit company resources to solve the problem.

Important Note:

You may also use the Operations Plan to write out directions for complex events without going through the detailed problem solving steps above.

A good idea is to write an Operations Plan for conducting your annual inventory. This is a reoccurring complex event. Most likely, each year you have new people in key positions. You need to get people working on key tasks long before the inventory day. Write a detailed plan this year and next year will be easier as you just updated it with your lessons learned.

District Managers - require your store managers to write an Operations Plan for their annual inventory day. Have them share ideas. This will have a direct and positive impact on your reported shrink.

Griffin Gorge Associates
To Sell Merchandise At A Profit

OPERATION PLAN

The Operations Plan coordinates the efforts of the stakeholders and provides a common operating picture.

The Operation Plan must provide enough detail to get the tasks accomplished, yet allow flexibility for the stakeholders to make adjustments as the plan progresses.

1. Situation
Briefly describe the current conditions and circumstances that created the need for action.

   a. <u>Area</u>
Identify the stores / districts / states effected by this plan.

   b. <u>Stakeholders</u>
List all of the stakeholders effected by the plan.

   c. <u>Assumptions</u>
Reasonably believe will happen or reasonably believe is true - but not confirmed. Often this is an expected future event.

2. Mission
In one paragraph, state the who, what, when, where and why.

3. Execution

   a. Leader's Intent
State the intent of the leader initiating this action.

     (1) <u>Task & Purpose</u>
State WHAT are you doing and WHY are you doing it.

     (2) <u>Goal</u>
State the desired outcome - be specific by using a measurable.

   b. Phases
Divide the plan into phases. For each phase state what defines the start and end. List some key actions and what the intent is. Be brief; limit each to one paragraph.

   c. Timeline
List all of the significant dates in sequential order.

   d. Specific Tasks
List tasks that are specific to an individual or small group. Think Ying-Yang. If you have Store 1 work with District 1; place a task for each.

   e. Common Tasks
List additional tasks that apply to all or most of the stakeholders.

MET 10: Problem Solving

4. Administrative & Logistic Information
List:
   Funding
   Resources available
   Constraints
   Personnel concerns
   Logistics

5. Communications
List the points of contact for key stakeholders:
   name
   position
   telephone
   email
   address

    SIGNATURE BLOCK
This person must have authority over all of the people tasked.

Now we will fill out an Operations Plan for our problem. For the sake of brevity and trees, this is very light on details. The intent is to show you how this flows.

The leadership provided additional guidance at the end of the Decision Brief. They stated the proposed COA will only be tested in District 1. Also, they directed the targeted District receive an additional 10% of the merchandise over last year.

LETTERHEAD

OPERATIONS PLAN: "SEASONAL MERCHANDISE"
DATE: AUGUST 30, 2010

1. Situation
Describe what event occurred to bring on the current problem.
The retail stores had excessive clearance merchandise at the end of the previous season. The buyers got significant discounts when purchasing in higher volume. However, the discounts were offset by increased leftover at the end of the season. Plans developed by the buyers and vendors for sales strategies were not thoroughly communicated to the stores. This resulted in the stores not selling the volume required to turn an acceptable profit.

    a. <u>Area</u>
District 1, to include stores # 1, 2, 3 and 4.

    b. <u>Stakeholders</u>
        Buyers
        Vendors
        Store Managers
        Salesman

    c. <u>Assumptions</u>
The market conditions will not change significantly next season.

2. MISSION
The buyers will coordinate with the stores in District 1 to execute a comprehensive plan to sell through the seasonal merchandise in order to increase regular sales and reduce markdowns associated with excess inventory at the end of the season.

3. EXECUTION
Note how these have changed from the Guidance Brief and the Decision Brief. They are now looking at how to solve the problem whereas before we were looking to find the problem and develop a COA.

MET 10: Problem Solving

a. Leader's Intent
State the intent of the leader initiating this action.
Buyers will coordinate with the stores in District 1 to increase the sales of the seasonal merchandise at regular prices during the season.

(1) Task & Purpose
State WHAT are you doing and WHY are you doing it.
Increase seasonal sales and reduce the amount of clearance inventory in the stores at the end of the season // in order to increase sales & profits while minimizing the amount of money lost through markdowns.

(2) Goal
State the desired outcome - be specific by using a measurable.
An increase in sales and profit for the season. Success is defined as having less than 5% of the merchandise being sold at clearance.

b. **Phases**
Divide the plan into phases. For each phase state what defines the start and end. List some key actions and what the intent is. Be brief; limit each to one paragraph.

Generally this will be as follows:

(1) Phase 1: The initial coordination among the stakeholders.
Starts upon publication of this Operation Plans and ends on November 1. The Buyers will conduct meetings with the DM, Store Managers and other select store staff to discuss the intent/plans for the next season merchandise buys. The vendors will provide guidance on merchandising and tactics to sell through. The Advertising Dept will coordinate efforts with the vendors and DM.

(2) Phase 2: The stage is being set for action.
Starts on November 1 and ends on April 1. The buyers will work with the DM and store staff for training sessions. The Advertising Dept will establish advertising events. The vendors will send representatives to each store. Merchandise arrives at stores.

(3) Phase 3. The execution. *The event happens here.*
Starts on April 1 and ends on June 30. The buyers and DM monitor sales to determine if the stores are on track to meet the goals. Stakeholders make notes for improvements.

(4) Phase 4. The post event actions. Starts on June 30 and ends on August 15. Stores shift to clearance of leftover goods. Buyers, Vendors, DM and selected store staff conduct a review to record successes and failure in the Operations Plan. A review is conducted to determine if the plan is continued or expended for next season.

c. Timeline

List all of the significant dates in sequential order.

2017
August 30   Publish the Plan
October 1   Buyers negotiate next season purchases

2018
March 1- 16   Merchandise ships to stores
March 2-20   Stores set up selling floor
April 1 - June 30   Season
July 1   Begin end of season clearance

d. Specific Tasks

List tasks that are specific to an individual or small group. Think Ying-Yang. If you have Store 1 work with District 1; place a task for each. Organize the list in accordance to the company hierarchy.

This is only for people you have authority to task. We will need Vendors to do things, but we cannot directly task them in this Operations Plan. Vendor taskings, or requirements, will be noted in the contract with them. The Task would be for the Buyer include it in the contract.

Try not to get too far into the weeds for the lower echelons. Here, we direct a Store to do something. Let the store manager decide how they will actually execute the action. This allows flexibility, saves you time, and puts some trust in your subordinates.

(1) <u>BUYERS</u>

(a) Coordinate with Vendor A to have seasonal items discounted in a linear regression matrix based on volume and margins. Get approval from VP prior to signing the contract.

(b) In Phase 1, meet with District 1 Manager to solicit suggestions for purchases.

(2) DISTRICT 1

    (a) Approve Store 1's training plan.

    (b) In Phase 1, meet with Buyers to provide suggestions for purchases.

(3) STORE 1

    (a) Provide training to all stores in District 1 between January 2 and March 15. Training must be approved by District 1. Coordinate directly with the other stores for training location/dates.

    (b) Host the review meeting NLT December 27.

(4) STORES 2 and 3

    (a) Coordinate directly with Store 1 to receive required training.

e. Common Tasks
List additional tasks that apply to all or most of the stakeholders.

    (1) All travel requests must be submitted through the District Manager to the Main Office.

    (2) Copies of trip reports will sent to the VP NLT five days after travel.

    (3) All stakeholders will attend the review meeting on {date} at STORE 1; exceptions must be approved by the VP.

4. Administrative & Logistic Information
List:
*   Funding*
*   Resources available*
*   Constraints*
*   Personnel concerns*
*   Logistics*

    a. Overtime will be authorized for staff working on this event.

    b. Travel budget will not exceed $10,000.

5. Communications
List the points of contact for key stakeholders.

James Greene
Seasonal Merchandise Buyer
(555) 514 8930
James@mailme.com
Home Office

Gary Barney
District 1 Manager
(555) 415-0398
Gary@mailme.com
Fairport Store

SIGNATURE BLOCK
Get the signature of the person you gave the briefings to. This person must have authority over all of the people tasked. In this example, the VP will sign.

Look at some of the good things that come out of this plan:

- The leadership is aware of what is happening, has provided guidance and allowed you to commit resources.

- The leadership can integrate this plan into the larger strategic goals/objectives of the company.

- There is a clear direction on the COA being taken.

- The stakeholders had the opportunity to express their needs and concerns. This leads to buy-in from them.

- The stakeholders know specifics on what they need to do and when they need to do it. Yet, they have some flexibility in how they accomplish their tasks.

- The stakeholders know their limitations and authorizations.

- You have saved the company a lot from wasted man-hours.

- The stakeholders have direction and can head off without a lot of additional discussion.

- You company is headed towards a selling season with the real expectation to increase sales and profit.

11. IMPLEMENT THE PLAN

Now you have a plan, with details, approved by the VP. The hard part is completed. But success will only come if you properly implement the plan. COMMUNICATE, COMMUNICATE, COMMUNICATE the plan to the lowest level.

    a. <u>Disseminate it</u>. Send the plan out to all the people and sections that will need to view it. The more people that get it, the better.

    b. <u>Validate it was received</u>. Do not just trust the plan got disseminated. There are people out there that do not like to pass information. You need to validate that the plan is out to those involved.

    c. <u>Get their plan backbrief</u>. The key people need to provide you with a backbrief. In a backbrief, the person validates they understand the plan and provides you with their plan. The manager for Store 1 needs to brief you on their plan to conduct the training.

    d. <u>Validate actions are being taken</u>. As the plan progresses, it is important to validate all the actions are being completed by the suspense date. **It is poor leadership to publish a plan and not do anything to enforce it.** Someone is bound to miss a suspense for a number of reasons. Be up front with them and let them know the secondary effects of not completing the action.

    e. <u>Update any company policies/guidance</u>. You have embarked on a new way of doing business. There might be some policies and guidance that will need to be updated.

    f. <u>Follow-up</u>. Make sure you flag some of the actions for follow-up. This shows the stakeholders your level of concern for the plan. It will also give you the opportunity to listen to concerns and ideas people are sure to have.

    g. <u>Refine</u>. Be ready to refine the plan as events progress and change. Do not continue to invest in something that is not working. Caution - significant changes will need to be vetted back through the VP.

12. CONCLUSION

Many intelligent individuals are working out there in retail, trying to solve the problems of the world. Once you learn the best way to solve problems, you, as a leader, will be effectively guiding the resources of your stores toward greater sales and profit.

Proper decision making skills will separate the professionals from the wing-nuts.

    a. Bringing a problem and solution to your boss (focus on yourself)

You are a leader in your field. You find a problem - go through the problem solving process and bring your boss solutions that will turn into a profit.

    b. You are able to focus your resources.

You have pinpointed a problem in your business. You have carefully focused resources to get it corrected. You have directly influenced your sales/profit.

    c. Reduction of problems.

Before, every six months you were spending time trying to figure out what to do with excess inventory. Now those days are gone. When you were "solving" that reoccurring problem you were not doing something else. Now you can go do something else.

    d. Personal life applications.

A young lady, Kim Polk, needed to make a life changing decision. She was a Soldier just back from a deployment and had earned her GI Bill to attend college. She needed to choose her course of study, but was torn between two choices.

She had a passion for photography but knew there were better career earning opportunities if she took business. She went through the Army's problem solving process and made her decision in less than an hour.

She sketched out some Facts & Assumptions. She listed 5 criteria and weighted them. She built a DECMAT and saw the answer. She built criteria on cost (one was cheaper), enjoyment of the work, earning prospects, career growth, and potential location.

She chose business for the earnings but ended up taking some photography courses to gain better enjoyment in her hobby.

Work an extra hour today to save a whole lot of time later.

MISSION ESSENTIAL TASK 11
ETHICS

1. INTRODUCTION

To establish a foundation of ethical behavior that reflects favorably upon yourself and your company. The Operational Level leaders must interact with a wide variety of people and scenarios. This includes the Strategic Office, your boss, Tactical Level subordinates, peers, customers, family and friends. There are many facets of your business that require a level of ethical behavior to maintain a long term and growing relationship. This MET centers on guiding Operational Level leaders to maintain a level of trust that fosters trustfulness in their practices. Successful leaders must hold a high accountability for ethical behavior in order for their business to achieve long term growth.

Ethics.... What defines the word? What does ethics mean in a retail store?

Defining ethics is like defining leadership. Ten people can give 25 different definitions and all of them are correct.

> **Ethics in a retail store means your customers, staff, peers and leadership trust you to do the right thing.**

Pretty ambiguous.

Supreme Court Justice Potter Stewart talked about defining pornography:

" I shall not today attempt further to define [pornography] and perhaps I could never succeed in intelligibly doing so. But I know it when I see it..."

Just about every company will have a short useless class on ethics; often prepared by a lawyer. At the end of the class you sign a sheet that has 5 things you cannot do and 5 things you must do. Sign at the bottom. If you ever fail, we will fire you. We are covered because we have your signature. Company is safe. Everyone go about your business.

Now those classes and papers do have a limited purpose. And little thought is needed on your part. But as Operational Level managers, as leaders, you must be prepared for the ethical decisions that are not covered in the class. In this Mission Essential Task, we try to set you up for making the right decisions in a questionable situation.

Good ethical foundations will set you and your company up for long term success.

So - how do we approach this ambiguous topic?

Building trust. The first step - you need to earn the reputation of being ethically sound. Can people trust you to make the right decision and do the right thing?

- Can your staff trust you to do the best for them?
- Can your customers trust you to provide goods at a reasonable price?
- Can your peers count on you to support them?
- Can your leadership trust you to run their stores?
- Can you trust your staff to do the same?
- Can you trust your leadership to support you?

Ethics is about building trust in everything you do.

2. ETHICS WITH YOUR STAFF

If you are being unethical with your staff, what are you going to get in return?

If you are having your employees clock out and keep them working, you are taking from them in a very unethical way. Short term - you just got a few more things done and did not pay them.

Long term losses:

-You just lost any loyalty from that employee. Having employees that lack any loyalty to your business just breeds a host of secondary problems.

-You develop a reputation that will drive the quality workers to your competition.

-You open yourself to be more susceptible to employee theft. You are literally stealing from your employees - a natural expectation from that is they will begin to steal from you and with some element of entitlement to do so.

Also - don't be an ass and take shortcuts that might be legal - but are unethical. There are stores out there that have employees clock in and out depending on the register sales. "Hey Jimmy, go clock out for 15 minutes until the sales catch up to match our hours." If you do that - you are an ass. Besides being unethical, that just shows poor planning, poor leadership and poor business sense.

Stores have been known to short employees on bonuses due. Sears once paid big ticket salesmen a commission. A hard charging young man, Dave, made a rather large sale of 100 generators to a business next door. His leadership did not pay the full commission because they felt a young man did not deserve to make that much in a week. Cheesy and unethical. Next time that customer came in for a big sale, Dave told them how to get it directly through the vendor.

Macy's would only pay salespeople for the hours they were scheduled. Those that stayed late to clean up the store at night did not get paid the extra 30 minutes. The employees started to fudge the timecards on other days to make up the difference. This created an adversarial and antagonistic relationship between the Operation Level and the Tactical Level.

> **When you treat your employees unethically,**
> **they will return the favor**
> **(and you may never know)**

3. ETHICS WITH YOUR CUSTOMERS

You are selling merchandise to your customer - and you are the expert. **Your customers need to trust you to make the best decision for them;** not just for you.

On the Operational Level, you need to establish standards for your staff to follow. The founders of Home Depot tell a great story about the ethics they made as a part of their company culture. A customer comes in stating they need a new faucet because theirs was leaking. Ready to spend $200, they start looking at the facets. The sales associate talks to the customer and ends up showing them how to fix the old one for $1.50.

The salesman very well could have sold the customer a new faucet. The customer expected that and would have left happy. But the salesman did the right thing; at the expense of a short term gain. He did this because that was the culture the Home Depot leadership sought to foster. When the CEO, Bernie Marcus, found out about this, he commented how that interaction, "reflects one of our core values: caring for the customer. Care for them today and they'll be back tomorrow." [11-1]

You do the same. Build your brand loyalty.

Sears came to a home to fix an ice buildup on the ice maker for a Kenmore refrigerator. The technician stated the entire ice making unit needed replacing. And, since it was old a refrigerator, the best option would be just to purchase a new one. The wife agreed and the technician left after giving her a coupon. She then looked up the problem on YouTube and found that someone else posted a way to fix this by putting a bent piece of coat hanger in the tube (it transferred the heat to prevent the ice build up). An honest company would know their product better and provide the cheaper fix.

You are the expert in the products and services you sell. Ethical behavior is conducting business with the customer in a way that is best for them. When your customers can trust you, they will be driving past your competitors to walk in your door.

A side effect of this, your staff will see this and offer you the same respect.

4. ETHICS WITH YOUR LEADERSHIP

Your purpose as a leader is to take the Strategic Level intent and turn it into action on the Tactical Level. Can your leadership trust you to make the right decisions for your company? They must have confidence in your technical skills and your ethical foundations. What does it mean, from their point of view, for you to have an ethical foundation?

Communicate information to your leaders in an honest way. Integrity is the right word.

> Be upfront. Tell it like it is.

> Be timely. Bad information does not get better with age. If you have a problem that is getting out of hand, let them hear it from you first.

> Don't Deceive. Sometimes you can make a factually correct statement but it is made to deceive or conceal the true picture. Communicate the real picture.

> Admit Mistakes. If you make a mistake, admit it and state what you are doing to fix it. If you never make mistakes you are either lying or a little weasel that never takes a chance - neither are good employees.

> Don't Blame. Never blame someone. Read Jocko's book. Take extreme ownership in your store.

> Ask. Ask questions when you are unsure of something.

> Follow Up. If you tell your leadership you are going to do something - do it. Building trust means your leadership knows if you say you are going to do something then they know you will.

> Discretion. If you have information that is confidential, your leadership must have faith that you will keep it that way. The worst people to trust are those that are your source of gossip.

> Communication. Answer the emails from your boss right away. As we said earlier, at least acknowledge receipt of the message even if you are not in the position to act. Then make sure you act as soon as possible. If your boss's boss emails you directly, acknowledge that and let your boss know about it.

5. ETHICAL BEHAVIOR IS A LEARNED TRAIT

Young, and impressionable, people will learn the boundaries of ethical behavior from the actions of their role models. This may be parents or more seasoned employees around them.

Bruce graduated high school and started working in the local maintenance shop.

Luke was a leader in the shop. Luke was a bully. He treated the other mechanics pretty poorly. He would view the shop equipment as his own. If he needed some supplies or tools, he saw no reason to buy what he could take. The shop morale fund managed by Luke was always short changed.

Bruce saw Luke as the correct way to behave, and embodied the ethos. Bruce saw Luke as someone to emulate. And, Bruce was going to do it to the next level. At least Luke was smart enough to keep things to a limit.

When Bruce started getting in trouble, he would lie, blame others and move on. Soon it got bad enough that termination papers were printed with his name at the top (see below).

Bruce left in a very angry fashion. The person he should have been angry at was Luke. Luke led him to honestly believe that unethical behavior was the correct multiple choice answer.

A hard working young lady in our store was caught under-ringing a couple making a large purchase. An audit showed she was doing this repeatedly on other sales to the same credit card to the tune of a few thousand dollars. Once we had the documentation and two police officers, she was confronted. She was a sobbing mess as she was cuffed and taken away.

The next day, the couple came in very upset. It turns out, the couple were her parents. They offered to make restitution if we would hire their daughter back. We told them their daughter would be making restitution as directed by the courts. Her termination was absolutely non-negotiable (We then let the police know about the parents being co-conspirators).

This young lady has a felony record because of the situation her parents put her in. She was pressured by the two people who should have been a positive influence in her life. But what if she never got caught? How would she be acting in other situations? How many times did her parents make her do other morally corrupt and illegal things? Did the conviction shift the family morals to make this a positive lesson?

6. ETHICS IS NOT ABOUT FOLLOWING THE RULES

As a leader, you will be in situations where breaking the rules becomes the best ethical choice.

A District Manager had about 20 maintenance shops across New York State. Heavy vehicle maintenance shops supporting customer fleets. They had a "rule" that the mechanics, or anyone, were not permitted to spend the night in the shop.

One night, this guy Munn - a great guy from Kingston - stayed in the shop working until 10pm. The customer had a dozen or so vehicles heading out at daybreak. Munn wanted to make sure everything was set. Munn lived almost two hours away. He wanted to be there when the customer came in for the trucks. Instead of driving home, he spent the night in the shop.

Simple math - leave at the shop at 10pm. Get home at midnight. Feed the dogs, have a snack and asleep by 1am. Up at 2:30am. Let the dogs out, grab a cup of coffee. On the road by 3am. In the shop at 5am. That sucks. Dangerous actually, considering the possibility of falling asleep while drive at 70 miles per hour.

Munn broke the rules. He spent the night in the shop. His supervisor allowed it. Anyone looking at that - any reasonable person - would agree that Munn and his supervisor did the right thing. Admirable in fact.

There is the gray area. This is the toughest because a reasonable person could argue for either choice. As a leader, you need to make the choice that is best for the organization as a whole.

Vinny got kicked out of his house. He failed on the part where you need to keep your life in focus (Mission Essential Task 12 of our program). Our founding fathers said we are all created equal. We are equal in regards to our inalienable rights. Not all equal in regards to levels of intelligence. Vinny was very unequal. Now he was on the street. His supervisor let him stay in the shop for a couple of weeks until he found an apartment. Right - maybe not. Wrong - maybe not. His leadership turned an eye. For almost a year after that - when the supervisor had a job nobody wanted to do, he went to Vinny. Vinny paid for rent in a different way.

The supervisor made the best choice for the organization. Had he not helped Vinny out, he would have most likely lost him as an employee. A dim witted but otherwise capable employee. The end result was a productive employee was retained. Vinny and the other employees saw their leadership as supportive. The supervisor increased his staff's loyalty to the organization.

Then there was Bruce (same as above). Bruce was a fool. He showed up to the shop around midnight with one of the other mechanics. Both drunk. With a prostitute. They took the shop ATV out on a joy ride. The ATV flipped and the other kid had his head crushed. The other kid almost died. Right? - no. Wrong - absolutely. This was definitely not in the gray area. Bruce was given the opportunity to find another job better suited for his skill set.

When a situation arises, just ask the simple question - does it sound right? Most likely that will be your answer.

MET 11: Ethics

7. WELLS FARGO - A CASE STUDY (11-2 to 11-6)

Let's take the sections covered above and look at a case study.

When the leadership in a company displays, and even promotes, unethical behavior, a host of bad consequences will emerge. Unfortunately, it may take years for the problem to manifest to full discovery.

Wells Fargo is an ethically challenged company.

They chose to excel profits on the short run over any long term game. They pressured their front end tellers and branch managers to open accounts and charge extra fees - at any cost. A customer comes in to open a single checking account. A week later they have three other savings accounts - all with some type of fee.

They were literally stealing from their customers. Tellers and branch managers that spoke up were terminated.

This game went on for years. It became the cultural norm for Wells Fargo employees to dream of news ways to rip off their customers. The behavior became woven into the fabric of the organization. Those that ripped the most got rewarded.

Let's look at the ramifications from this ethically challenged behavior.

First - Their short term profits were up. They had some very productive branches. Shareholders love that part. Employees are happy with the bonuses.

Second - The good employees speak up. They are terminated. The company actively, as a matter of policy, terminates what would be defined as a good employee.

Third - It breeds a selection process where the branch managers are looking to hire other ethically challenged employees.

Fourth - A Wells Fargo branch is staffed by employees being coached and pressured to steal from the customers. This begs the question - are they also stealing from the company?

Fifth - Some customers begin to notice the fees. Some will complain and get the funds returned (after a fight). Others quietly (or loudly) switch banks.

Sixth - The branches become more brazen in their actions. The customers are leaving. The bad employees must step up the game to stay in the game.

Seventh - This business model becomes unsustainable. Things come crashing down. Deals are made on the Strategic - Political Level. Fines are paid.

Eight - Wells Fargo is struggling to keep branches open. They are now closing many of their branch offices.

Ninth - Now what kind of talent can they hire? It is well known that they were firing honest workers. They only talent they get are those who can't get work elsewhere - or those who are getting paid a premium.

Today, the leadership at Wells Fargo is struggling to regain their stature. They have a long uphill battle to change their internal culture and customer perception.

In the short run - ethically challenged companies can make a good profit.

In the long game - a company with a strong ethical compass will grow and thrive. They will attract the talent for employees and the trust of their customers.

8. THE TOUCHY SUBJECT OF YOUR STAFF AND ETHICS

OR - Penises, Vaginas and Hormones

When you mix these up with a glass of wine you can have a very good life. People eat. People sleep. People have sex. It is natural. It happens. You cannot stop it. It will happen when you mix people up in a group and keep them together for more than a week. It is what sustains life to the next generation.

Mixing these in your store does not make for a good work environment for a whole lot of reasons. You are a leader for your company. Employees notice their leaders. If you are banging someone on your staff, everyone will know before you put your clothes back on. You will lose the trust of your staff - how can you make good decisions for them? Every decision you make regarding the employee you are banging will be viewed with suspicion regardless of how sound it might otherwise be.

Your leaders will lose trust in your ability to make the right decisions for their company.

You are working with a variety of people every day. Some of them you are spending most of your waking hours with. You get to know them very well. To deny that attractions will happen is to deny your humanity.

You are a leader and you are the adult in the situation.

- Don't go fishing off the company pier.
- Don't dip your pen in company ink.

If you do find yourself in a situation where BOTH of you have strong feeling towards each other, deal with it appropriately. One of you move to another position or to another company. Don't deny your attraction if that is truly something both of you want. Just make sure it gets put in the right context.

MET 11: Ethics

You are the leader - understand you need to respect those around you by making sure it is an environment people feel good about working in.

Absolutely one of the saddest moments in my working career was when Wendy and I were parting ways. She worked for me in a store. Wendy was a very attractive lady that worked evenings with us after her regular job. She was always walking around with a gorgeous smile. Very friendly and great with the customers. Very considerate employee. I was leaving to go work at another store. On my last day she came up and thanked me. She said I was the first guy she every worked for that did not sexually harass her. That is sad. I did not know how to reply to that. Thank you for appreciating me for not sexually harassing you???

I wonder how she felt coming into work at other jobs knowing, expecting, to be sexually harassed. And it happened everywhere. When a lady working with customers smiles - it is because that is her job - not because she wants to roll in the hay with you. This becomes more than some type of mutual attraction - it becomes an abuse of power and control.

More than Wendy's bosses being unethical; where were the other leaders? It is most likely that other leaders along the way knew what was happening with Wendy and did nothing to properly address it. If you become aware of a situation like that, you have an obligation to act. Most likely you will hear unsubstantiated rumors first. Rumors are bad sources of information, but they are smoke that can lead you to a fire. The best way to address a rumor would be to sit down and talk to Wendy. Talk directly to the person who is the reported target of the harassment. Then, if you suspect there is something amiss, you must go to your Human Resource representative. If a problem is discovered, you must not go off on your own. Also, document your conversations by writing good notes. The key point is you must act to properly address a serious issue.

It is not a one way street. You might find some of your staff flirting with you - or more. You are the leader. Be the adult. Only you can make the right decision on how to handle that situation. A subtle indication of "not happening" must be communicated. Avoid being alone with them. Be blunt if it does not stop. But don't take the wrong action.

A tougher position - what to do when two of your subordinates are teaming up. If it is a clear supervisor-subordinate role you need to end it fast. Move one if you need to. You handle it the way you see fit - but our advice is to always be informal first. These matters are always different and always tricky. Don't be afraid to seek out advice from a peer or your boss. Just remember - by going to your boss you are raising the stakes. Ask too many peers about it and you start the rumor mill.

If two subordinates are dating and there is no supervisory relationship - let it go. Just get concerned if it starts to affect their work performance.

9. VENTING & GOSSIP

People need to talk. We are social creatures that thrive on interactions with others. An important part of our social interactions is being able to vent about issues and problems. Venting is actually a healthy function when it is done in the right context. It can help us with analyzing a problem and developing solutions. Venting about a problem can help us put order to the issue by walking through the steps.

Venting does not always require a solution; sometimes you just need to get it off your chest. When an issue stresses us, talking about it can relieve some of that stress. A person normally feels a sense of relief after venting.

Venting needs to be done in the right context. A good way is to have a partner outside of the workplace that you can open up to. They are often someone you can express commentary and opinions to with no repercussions. A good partner can offer outside perspectives on solutions.

You should also seek to have a peer at work you can vent to. Someone you have confidence in that they will not go around repeating what you confide. You can be the one they vent to. This person works in the same environment which allows them to have some insights on solutions.

You do not vent to your subordinates. You do not vent around the coffee pot. You do not vent to everyone who walks into your office. You not vent to everyone who calls you. And **never** vent with an email.

Venting placed in the wrong context fosters an unhealthy workplace. It creates a negative atmosphere. You are a leader. First, you need to set the example. Second, you need to enforce the standards for your subordinates.

Gossip in any form will create a bad environment. Many good people have had their careers harmed by unfounded salacious rumors. Gossip does nothing but harm to your company.

Without any constraints, people love to spread rumors. There is an old saying: "If I get promoted, some people might not know for months. If I get fired for stealing, everyone will know before lunch."

Do you have someone who consistently comes to you with the latest gossip and innuendos? Then you just found someone you can never trust.

If you want to have an ethically sound and healthy workplace, you MUST squash the rumor mills. When you hear people talking gossip, steer the conversation to another direction. Have talks with your subordinate leaders during your mentoring sessions.

Set the example - always. If you vent to the wrong crowd, or spread gossip, your peers and subordinates will follow.

10. DIVERSITY

In Mission Essential Task 2 Staff, we discussed racism in regards to building your workforce. In Ethics, we need to expand on this a little.

Diversity is having a store where the **leadership, staff, customers** and **community** share the same balance of race, age, religion, ethnicities, gender and whatever other grouping you can identify. This directly ties in with building trust. When someone from the outside looks at your organization and sees true diversity, they naturally gain trust that you are doing the right thing. When they fail to see diversity, your excuses will not overcome their distrust.

Many organizations try to build a culture that will foster equal treatment for all categories of diversity. Resources for policies, programs and training are sunk into creating the culture. Yet, many times, the intended results do not manifest; however the leadership feels good about themselves and the lawyers feel insulated from lawsuits. This begs the question on why policies and sound guidance to not always produce the results. An entire book could be written on this topic and this is not that book.

So, what can the retail Operational Level leaders do to foster diversity that goes beyond what your organization provides?

First, look at the make-up of the leadership you supervise, your staff and your customers and the community you are in. Is there a balance? If yes, it means you must be doing things right, even if it is a subconscious action.

If the answer is an unbalanced mix, then how do you ethically shift that balance? The wrong answer is to just hire the next ten people of the unrepresented group. That action is just as bad.

A good place to start is to discuss the imbalance you found with your Human Resources representative along with your boss. They can be a great resource of information and may actually offer a path to the solution.

Find ways to recruit from areas that have the under-represented population you are looking for. Suppose your staff is an all young under thirty group and your community has a large older over 50 crowd. You can shape this by recruiting from the senior communities in the area.

You can be blunt and ask direct questions. If you have a lot of females on your staff and only one in a leadership position, sit down and ask her about how to shift the balance. If you have a lot of Hispanics on staff and none in a leadership position, sit down and talk to them. You may be surprised at the answers.

Look at your customers coming in the door. Do they represent the population diversity in your community? If you see that there is a segment of the community that is not shopping in your stores - you just might be missing an opportunity to grow your business.

The point is - you need to occasionally review the actual diversity statistics for your stores and take actions to keep it diverse. **Good programs and policies are not the measure of an organization's success in diversity.**

By creating diversity in your workforce, you are tapping into a pool of talent. By shaping the diversity of your customers, you are increasing your sales.

11. CONCLUSION

Ethics is about doing the right thing. It is gaining the confidence of your leadership, staff, peers, customers, and family to trust that you are making the right decisions. People can trust that you are communicating honestly.

Ethical behavior is the correct path to the long term growth of your business.

MISSION ESSENTIAL TASK 12
FOCUS ON YOURSELF

1. INTRODUCTION

To maintain your mental and physical self at a high standard. You are a significant asset to your company. They have invested resources into training you. There has been a level of practical experience invested in you. With that, the company has placed a lot of trust in you to perform your duties which includes stewardship over millions of dollars in assets and the trust to operate their business profitably. This MET centers on your responsibility to take good care of a key company asset. Properly taking care of yourself will put you in a position to increase revenues and profit.

You are important. Your care is a Mission Essential Task.

You are a leader running a store or set of stores that generate millions of dollars in revenue. You supervise a workforce that counts on you to keep the business viable so they have jobs. Your Strategic Office counts on you to make sound decisions on their behalf.

You need to count on yourself to take care of you. If you are neglecting yourself, then your work and personal life will suffer negative consequences.

People who have a positive outlook, are well nourished, exercise, are mentally fit, and engage in learning perform better at their professions and personal relationships.

This is about lifestyles, not just good days and bad days.

2. POSITIVE OUTLOOK

There are a lot of skills people can learn to do a variety of jobs. As Commander Ettrich said, these are intelligent people who just need to be trained. But it is extraordinarily difficult to train someone to have a positive outlook.

<u>What is a positive outlook?</u>

Someone who sees a good opportunity in adversity. Someone who works through difficult problems with the honest conviction that a better result lies ahead.

They tend to rise to better positions in their fields and have a higher quality of satisfaction in their relationships.

They tend to take calculated risks with the prospect that there will be a better outcome.

<u>A negative outlook</u> is demonstrated by someone who views events around them as an ever increasing downward spiral. Any action is sure to lead to a worse outcome.

Their lack of career progression is the result of some ass-kisser beating them out on a promotion or a consequence of ignorance by their leadership.

They shy away from taking calculated risks because they do not trust that the outcome will lead to something better.

There is this guy Paul. He was always too smart to finish the college he started. He works in junior positions; never progressing far. This is because his leadership consists of a tub of morons with Masters Degrees and know nothing of how things really work. They just make a ton more money and work less hours, but he could definitely do their jobs with greater precision.

Sorry Paul. Your statements prove they did the right thing. They put themselves in a position to work less and get paid more. Tell me again who is smarter?

The agnostic sits in the middle. To them, life is just there. If they get promoted at work - good. If they never move on to better things - that's good too.

To the agnostic, taking a calculated risk means expending energy; which is just too much to do.

You need to reach inside yourself and develop a positive outlook. We can tell you the WHAT and WHY in this workbook, the HOW lies somewhere else.

Jocko Willink best describes the importance and the how of a positive outlook in his book, "Extreme Ownership". Read it.

Go to Youtube and look up Jocko Motivation "GOOD" (From Jocko Podcast)
A fantastic motivational talk that is less than three minutes.

3. COMMUNICATE CLEARLY

You will be sending out written emails every day.

Write clearly. Review your emails before sending. Texts with auto-correct can cause issues.

If you take the time to communicate clearly, with well written sentences, you will be more effective.

4. ENGAGE IN LEARNING

If you are running a store or managing a group of stores, we suspect you might have some level of intelligence and education.

Education is a lifelong event that is not limited to formal classes in a University.

A great way to expand your experience is to read about others in their books. Check out your local library; wander around and pick up whatever interests you. The book sucks? Just return it and find another one.

The public library in Schenectady, NY has an annual book sale. You pay five bucks for a brown paper grocery bag. They have tables of books set about the sidewalks out front. Fill up the bag with what your heart desires. You are sure to walk away with enough books to last a year. Find out if one of your local libraries do the same.

In Mission Essential Task 4 Community, we discussed the importance of reading the local news and other periodicals to learn about the world around you. These count as learning.

Check out your local community college. Often, they will offer courses to non-students in a variety of subjects. The price and quality are the best value you will find anywhere.

There are some fantastic resources online that will offer self-paced courses for a wide range of topics. Khan Academy is world class and free (www.khanacademy.org). There are some other very good places to find free online courses.

Expanding your knowledge will bring a host of benefits in your life.

Your mind is a muscle; exercise it.

5. WELL NOURISHED

Your body is a machine like any mechanical device with an engine. It needs to be well oiled and fed the right fuel to run.

You need to work on a healthy balanced diet. Make it a lifestyle. You will have more energy and think better. You will live longer, take less pills and just feel better.

Diet means more than just watching your weight. It means getting the right nutrients to your body while avoiding the fuels that gum it up.

There are many diet programs out there with varying success rates. You can try different ones to find the diet that gets you feeling the best.

A general rule is to polish off a good variety of fruits and vegetables. Meats and dairy keep the pace going. Drink juices and water.

Avoid processed foods. Potato chips, ring dings, cookies, ice cream, candy bars, and cakes should be very limited to the point of just three times a month for any combination of them. Avoid processed meats and other processed foods. Cut out the sugar drinks and soda. Stop adding salt to anything. You need salt but the American diet has enough salt added to food that you do not need more except in cases where you are being physically exerted for hours.

Read labels on the foods. American grocery stores have a huge variety of foods to choose from. However, this is a free country. There are no laws requiring them to put the nutritious foods up front. Read labels: Plum juice can be labeled as Cranberry Juice as long as there is a splash of cranberry.

You should not need a multi-vitamin if your diet is balanced. You may need supplements for specific elements your individual body needs.

There have been many studies on nutrition that seem to contradict each other. The most likely answer lies with the organization that paid for the study. Use your common sense with the above tips and will see a significant improvement.

Just making these adjustments will show results in a few months. You should not expect to see results after just a few days.

6. EXERCISE

Inge and her husband retired twenty years ago. She rides her bike with the objective to do 1000 miles every few months. She is in great shape and takes no medications. Her friends told her it is dangerous to ride a bike at her age. She replied that is more dangerous not to ride a bike.

Active people have less joint pain and take less medications.

Exercise does not mean doing a Navy SEAL workout at 5am every morning with Jocko. Exercise can often mean just getting out and moving.

Get involved with some yoga classes. Join the YMCA and sign up for some of the activities there. Many people join gyms for a New Year's resolution then drift away from it in the Spring. Good for them for trying. But you do not need to be working out in a gym to get your exercise in.

Change your lifestyle to conduct many of your daily activities in a way that involve some small acts of exercise.

When going up a few flights, take the stairs instead of the elevator. Walk the 1/2 mile to the store instead of driving. Take the long way around when walking to someplace. Take an evening stroll for a mile or two.

Engage in some physical activities that can benefit you in other ways. Chop a load of fire wood. Shovel the snow instead of using a snow blower. Rake the yard by hand.

The important thing is just to get that body moving. Do something every day to get that blood flowing for just a few minutes.

7. MENTALLY FIT

Mentally fit means taking appropriate breaks from work and getting yourself refreshed. When you refresh your mind, your productivity and quality of work will increase.

    A. <u>Take breaks during your workday</u>. When you eat lunch, step out of the store and go have lunch at a park bench. If you have a tough time doing that on a day, at least walk down the street to get a cup of coffee or tea. Just taking a minute to catch your breath will make you feel better.

    B. <u>Step away on at least one of your days off each week</u>. In retail it's tough to get away from the store on your days off. There are always some questions or actions that need your great advice. Reserve one day per week for no calls or emails.

    C. <u>Check out on long weekends and fully disengage for vacations</u>. This requires some good trust in your subordinates to take the reins. It also takes some trust from your boss to allow you to pass important decisions. Cultivate that trust. When someone takes a vacation and fully checks out, their level of productivity noticeably increases. The military found out that during long combat tours, the leaders that took their full R&R in the middle of their deployment performed much better. The leaders that did not take R&R looked physically worse and made bad decisions. Learn from them and do your store a favor - check out on occasion. Breaks improve mental fitness.

    D. <u>Take up a hobby:</u>

Fishing	Hiking
Hunting	Target shooting
Sewing	Solving math problems
Crochet	Cooking
Building doll houses	Volunteer at a food bank
Gardening	Volunteer at a local playhouse
Woodworking	Play a musical instrument
Bowling	Ballroom dancing
Softball team	Photography
Building train sets	Make a dress
Build model airplanes	Golf
Sailing	Landscaping

Hobbies are a great way to re-set your mind after a long day. They can give you a sense of personal accomplishment and reward. Some hobbies can contribute to your physical health. Some help out humanity. Some will allow you to meet new people. Some are just mindless activities that offer you a chance to relax.

You can try one and stop if you do not enjoy it.

The point is you need to move your mind to a place other than work. It will produce positive long term results in your work performance and health.

8. GROOMING

Grooming matters. Let's face it, nobody wants to work with someone who smells, has nasty hair or dirty clothes.

In addition to your work force, you face customers every day. In a real sense, your selling floor is a stage. Be the actor in proper costume. And that means being well groomed.

We had a General once who was notoriously a pain in the ass for making sure all the Soldiers and Airmen wore their uniform just right. He was at the St Patrick's Day parade in New York City and chastised a Captain for not correcting one of his Soldiers that had a boot lace sticking out. The Captain said sorry but there are just too many scantily clad women to notice a boot lace. Rumor has it that was the only time the General laughed.

Anyway - the General's underlying point was a leader must take care and pride when getting dressed in the morning. He held the belief that if a leader did not take care of the little things like getting dressed, how competent were they at their other tasks?

You need to take time in the morning to get ready for you day. Clean well pressed clothes. Hair combed and finger nails trimmed. Shoes shined, teeth brushed and nose hairs plucked. Every Army barracks has a mirror by the door. Young Soldiers are trained to look at themselves before leaving. Do the same.

Studies show that well groomed and well postured people have more positive encounters with others. When you are on the selling floor dealing with an irate customer, if you look the part, it will play into your advantage for gaining calm in the situation. When you are directing your staff, you are setting an example without saying anything.

When you are interacting with the Strategic Office, you will have a subliminal edge in gaining their confident that you are the right choice to be out there leading the Operational Level.

9. RELATIONSHIPS

Everyone has some type of relationships in their personal lives. Relationships involve your interactions with friends, family, acquaintances, and intimate partners. Every situation is as different as a shuffled deck of cards. Relationships will change as we mature and move around this planet. They shift based on emotions, geography, interests and competing time requirements.

Some people choose to have many friends, some just a few. Some people hang out with just family, or just select members from one side of the family. Some hang out in bars and some in the library.

Whatever you preference is, your relationships with other people is what life is really about. It is what makes us human. Spend time to cultivate the relationships that are important to you. This is important for you to grow as a person.

Employees that have built strong relationships on the outside perform better. Employees whose personal lives are train wrecks will normally bring those issues to the workplace in some form. By keeping your personal affairs in order, your work performance will gain.

10. PERSONAL FINANCES

You are responsible for the finances in your store. Millions of greenbacks will pass through your stewardship. You take pride in your skills to manage a high volume business that needs to show a profit. Your financial agility keeps America running.

You need to give yourself the same loving.

Poor finances are a leading cause of stress. Put yourself in a positive position. We do not offer financial advice - there are better trained folks for that. We do offer some solid tips that any financial advisor will agree with.

    A. <u>Live below your means</u>. Too many people live spending slightly more than they make; always expecting their pay will catch up. The pay never catches up. Review where you spend your money and cut back. Make it a habit to review all of your expenses annually with the intent to cut spending and increase savings.

    B. <u>Save</u>. Open a separate savings account and tuck a few bucks a week into it. Get it up to four times your monthly expenses. Life sucks sometimes. Have something for when you are in a crunch. AND needing the new computer is not crunch time.

    C. <u>IRAs</u>. Put money in a Roth or Traditional. Roth is better when you are in the lower half of middle aged. You work in retail. There are not exactly many (as in zero) retail companies that offer a retirement plan. Put money in here even if it hurts. The defined company sponsored retirement plans are fading fast in other industries. Those that do still offer them are cutting back. The City of Detroit cut the pensions of their already retired city employees. Many other towns followed. The best place for your retirement savings is in an account you have some control over. Just find a reputable financial institution.

    D. <u>Stand up to peer pressure</u>. You may have peers or family that will pressure you to buy things, go places and experience new wonders for the low price of a few grand. A Caribbean vacation is wonderful; but it is a poor investment (unless you own the resort). Peers making less than you will put the pressure on. You think if they can afford it, so can you. They have the best intentions to go have a good time with you at their side. Be smart. Be strong.

You work hard for your money. You are the one responsible to put your hard work into your future.

11. BUILD A PERSONAL SET OF GOALS, OBJECTIVES AND BATTLE RHYTHM

You need to provide sound guidance to yourself.

Following almost the same process as we covered in Mission Essential Task 1, set Goals, Objectives and a Battle Rhythm for you. As a retail business, "Selling Merchandise At A Profit" is a single and sufficient Goal.

You are more dynamic than a retail store could ever be.

Set a few long term Goals for yourself. These Goals are years or decades away from being reached. They become a way to guide your life activities. For many people, it could be a higher level degree you work on at night. A good Goal is writing out where you want to be financially. It would be very wise to make a career Goal. A real long term Goal would be crafting a lifestyle that incorporates a healthy activity or hobby.

Once you have those Goals, set a few Objectives for each. Writing out what actions you will do to move towards the Goal is essential. Unlike Mission Essential Task 1, it is not essential to draft full scale Action Plans for each of the Objectives (You can if you wish - it's a free country). You do not have a boss to approve these, but if you have a life partner the two of you should work on these together.

The Goals and Objectives will provide a sense of direction for your life. Now set a Battle Rhythm to keep you on track. A Battle Rhythm is a tool to keep stress out of your face. Plan out when you get the house chores done, build your hobbies and exercise routine into it. A semi-annual event is your vacation. Put long weekends in there. Take your personal Battle Rhythm and go into work with it. Nest it to your work Battle Rhythm to plan the time off. Bring to the boss. When you bring your boss a plan for all the long weekends and vacations - he will buy into your statement that you have a plan for the subordinates to pick up the slack.

12. CONCLUSION

Take good care of yourself and your family.

FOOTNOTES

(1-1) Stephen Stills, Rick Curtis, and Michael Curtis, *Southern Cross*, (Atlantic Records) September 1982.

(3-1) *Comcast* (The Economist) March 15, 2014

(3-2) Brad Reed, *Comcast Employees Explain Why Their Customer Service Is So Terrible* (bgr.com) July 16, 2014.

(3-4) Stephanie Mlot, *Comcast Is America's Most Hated Company* (PC Magazine) January 12, 2017.

(3-5) Khairie A, Comcast *Xfinity Review* (CreditDonkey.com) April 25, 2018.

(3-6) YELP reviews on Comcast rate 1 Star with 103 reviews, November 5, 2018.

(3-7) Khadeeja Safdar, *Stores That Track Your Returns* (Wall Street Journal) April 4, 2018.

(3-8) Erica E. Phillips, *Retailers Offer Myriad Returns Options to Retain Customers* (Wall Street Journal) December 26, 2017.

(3-9) Elizabeth Holmes, *Beware Signs That Say 'Final Sale'* (Wall Street Journal) August 3, 2016.

(3-10) Paul Ziobro, *Target Extends Return Window for Private Label Brands* (Wall Street Journal) March 18, 2015.

(3-11) Dennis Green, *L.L. Bean Just Changed Its Return Policy* (Business Insider) February 9, 2018.

(3-12) Marcus, Bernie & Blank, Arthur, *Built From Scratch* (Crown Business) 1999

(11-1) Marcus, Bernie & Blank, Arthur, *Built From Scratch* (Crown Business) 1999, pages 103-104

(11-2) *Wells Fargo Reports 1.4m Additional Fake Accounts* (The Economist) September 4, 2017

(11-3) *Wells Fargo's Q3 Profit Falls By 19% On Legal Costs* (The Economist) October 16, 2017

(11-4) Brian Mahany, *Wells Fargo Whistleblowers* (Mahany Law) August 25, 2018

(11-5) *Wells Fargo, Scrambling To Cut Costs And Offset Soaring Legal Expenses, Plans To Pull The Plug On 800 More Bank Branches By 2020* (CNN Money) January 12, 2018

(11-6) *Wells Fargo's Reputation Plummeted* (The Economist) September 7, 2017

(11-7) *After Wells Fargo Admitted Last Fall To Creating As Many As 2 Million Fake Accounts, Nearly Half A Dozen Former Employees Told CNN Money They Were Retaliated Against After They Tried To Stop These Illegal Tactics* (CNN Business) January 23, 2017

(11-8) *At An American Bank, Staff Found Dodgy Ways To Meet Targets Set By Higher-Ups* (The Economist) September 17, 2016

BIBLIOGRAPHY

Albright, Madeleine, *The Mighty and the Almighty* (Harper Collins) 2006

Carnegie, Dale, *The Quick and Easy Way to Effective Speaking* (Pocket Books) 1962

Gladwell, Malcolm, *Outliers* (Little, Brown) 2008

Langone, Kenneth, *I Love Capitalism* (Portfolio / Penguin) 2018

Marcus, Bernie & Blank, Arthur, *Built From Scratch* (Crown Business) 1999

Martinez, Arthur, *The Hard Road to the Softer Side* (Crown Business) 2001

McIntyre, Deni, *No Place Like Lowes* (Cliff Oxford) 1996

Nemeth, Charlan, *In Defense of Troublemakers* (Basic Books) 2018

Peters, Thomas & Waterman, Robert, *In Search of Excellence* (Warner Books) 1982

Powel, Colin, *My American Journey* (Ballantine Books) 1995

Willink, Jocko & Babin, Leif, *Extreme Ownership* (St Martin's Press) 2015

Open Source:

Center for Army Lessons Learned, *Military Decision Making Process (MDMP)*, No 15-06, March 2015

Department of the Army, *The Counseling Process*, ATP-6-22.1, July 2015

Joint Chiefs of Staff, *Joint Publication 5-0, Joint Planning,* 16 June 2017

SERVICES OFFERED BY GRIFFIN GORGE ASSOCIATES

Below is a list of the basic services offered by Griffin Gorge Associates. Please email us for the most current listing and pricing. GriffinGorge@mail.com

Seminar on the book - To Sell Merchandise At A Profit
This is a two day course, conducted at your location. Target audience is 10 students.

Planning
This is a two day course, conducted at your location. Target audience is 10 students We work with the students to write their Objectives, and outline Action Plans. Learn to develop a Battle Rhythm and set up a Continuity Binder. After the course, the Instructor will follow-up with the students, via email and telephone, for a six month period to track progress and provide additional mentoring.

Staff Development I
This one day course conducted at your location. Target audience is 20 students. We train your leaders on how to develop a staff that will grow your business. It is beneficial to have our course "Planning" as a prerequisite; but not required.

Staff Development II
This two day course conducted at your location. Target audience is 6 students. The first day covers the same material as Staff Development I. On the second day, the instructor works with the students to write staff development plans for their business.

Problem Solving & Decision Making
This two day course conducted at your location. Target audience is 10 students. On the first day, we go through the problem solving steps and decision making steps. On the second day, we take a real problem and walk you through the steps all the way to writing the plan.

Ethics Training
This four hour course conducted at your location. Target audience is 20 students. Designed to train leaders and engage them in discussions on how to bring ethical decision making and role modeling to your business.

Additional Retail Coaching & Support
We offer coaching and practical support for the following targeted subjects:
- Building an Operations Plan for Inventory Day
- Building a Continuity Binder
- Building a Community Binder
- Inventory Flow Management
- Floor Checklists

Mission Essential Task List Development
Our team will work with your Strategic Office to develop a METL set specific for your stores.

District Mentorship Program
A 10 month mentoring program for District Mangers. A Griffin Gorge instructor works directly with a District Manager in to put all the Key Elements of this book into action for their stores.

www.ingramcontent.com/pod-product-compliance
Lightning Source LLC
Chambersburg PA
CBHW021414210526
45463CB00001B/372